Ali, the Fighting Prophet

MUHAMMAD ALI (CASSIUS CLAY)

A Sporting Print

Ali, the Fighting Prophet

by Gilbert Odd

with a Foreword by Henry Cooper

Pelham Books - London

First published in Great Britain by
Pelham Books Ltd
52 Bedford Square
London WC1B 3EF
1975

ISBN 0 7207 0845 1

Printed in Great Britain by
Hollen Street Press Ltd at Slough
and bound by Dorstel Press at Harlow, Essex

Acknowledgements for photographs used in this book
are due to:
    Syndication International
    Associated Press
    Central Press
    Sport and General
    Alan Raymond

Foreword by Henry Cooper

This is a book about a remarkable man, not only a fine boxer, but an extrovert character who has brought such world-wide attention to himself that his name is almost a household word. As a public entertainer he has had few equals.

When I first knew him in 1963, he was Cassius Clay, an unbeaten 21-year-old scrapper with tremendous confidence and dedication; a born athlete, finely equipped both physically and mentally to become a great champion. He had marvellous legs that enabled him to move with the grace and speed of a ballet dancer, while his reflexes were fantastic. I doubt if there has been, or ever will be, a faster moving heavyweight. Opposing him was like boxing a shadow.

No enmity among fighters. Henry Cooper and Muhammad Ali in some clowning at a London reception in 1975.

The next time I met him, three years later, he had changed his name to Muhammad Ali, but was his same flamboyant self, if perhaps not quite so cocky. But he was just as fast and even more difficult to catch with a decisive punch, a man who had brought the art of self defense almost to perfection. I say, almost, because no one has taken so many liberties with the orthodox methods of protecting oneself as Ali. Even after all those years of fighting, he still has novice-like lapses when on the ropes or in a corner, and taken chances that make me shudder—yet gets away with them.

My friend, Gilbert Odd, has asked me to say how I rate Ali. Well, I don't share his claims to being The Greatest heavyweight of all time, but I do class him among the top five, including him with such notables as Jack Johnson, Jack Dempsey, Joe Louis and Rocky Marciano, each different in style, but all having greatness about them.

Ali tells us that he got the idea of calling himself The Greatest in imitation of a noted wrestler, Gorgeous George, who used this to good purpose as a publicity gimmick. Adopting the same idea is about the only non-original thing he has ever done. In everything else he is unique and I have a great admiration for him, even if he blows his top occasionally.

I have often been asked if, on the two occasions I fought him, he ever chatted me up as he did so many of his opponents. Actually, he never said a word, being, I imagine, too busily occupied in concentrating on what he was doing. I know I was gritting my teeth, determined to beat him, and you can't talk much in such circumstances.

I have known Gilbert throughout all my boxing days and ever since. He turns out a good book and this should be another winner, because he does know what he is writing about.

Introduction

The subject of this work needs no introduction. Under his real name, Cassius Clay, and his adopted name, Muhammad Ali, he is known throughout the universe, while in all the countries where there is television he has a vast audience—even including those who are not interested in professional boxing as such. No other man in the history of fist fighting, from the days of the redoubtable James Fig in 1720, has commanded more attention in a world-wide capacity as has this coloured Kentuckian, both in his undoubted genius in the ring and his powers of oration out of it. Of course, he has had the mediums of television, radio and films at his disposal, but the important point is that he has used these to full advantage. Since he first claimed public attention by winning gold at the Rome Olympics in 1960, he has rarely been out of the public limelight.

I never thought anyone would equal dynamic Jack Dempsey as a fighting machine until I saw Joe Louis, who to me was the complete box-fighter. No one, I imagined, would ever surpass the great Brown Bomber in skill and hitting power—and then came Clay, to embody all the assets of his predecessors, create a new look in ring warfare, and outdo every heavyweight champion of the past when it came to providing his own publicity. After watching, reporting and studying the Fight Game for the best part of a long life-time, knowing all the great ones, both in and out of the ring, I unhesitatingly agree that Cassius Clay (Muhammad Ali) has every right to style himself The Greatest.

He has had his bad moments, has suffered temporary humiliation and setbacks, yet has risen above every adversity with egotistical faith and supreme confidence in his mental and physical abilities. Brash—yes, arrogant—no. A ruthless conqueror—yes, a sadistic destroyer—no, even on one or two occasions when it may have seemed so. He is the clearest thinker among fighting men I have ever known, a fact fully emphasised in the manner in which he has stood up to specialist television interviewers.

Those who dislike his lengthy vocal outbursts and the derisive manner in which he denounces his opponents or his critics, should realise two things if they wish to try and understand the nature of this colourful character. First, he is an impulsive talker, who has never been quiet for any conscious length of time since he was first able to make himself understood. Second, he does not mean half of what he says, as the various quotes in this story testify. He has grown up physically, but at heart is still an eager,

THE YOUTHFUL CASSIUS CLAY
at the age of 20

THE MATURE MUHAMMAD ALI,
aged 28

boisterous, loquacious youngster, with strong beliefs and a great sense of moral values. He is also a master of the Noble Art of Self Defence, who has taken the ring against the toughest and hardest-hitting heavyweights in the world and reduced the majority of them to impotency without suffering any physical damage himself.

I am thankful that I was given the opportunity to see such an artist in action and to have had the opportunity of conversing with him—outside the ring!

GILBERT ODD
Northiam, 1975

1. Showman from Birth

According to Muhammad Ali (formerly Cassius Clay), he was destined to become a fighting man from babyhood, when he doubled up a tiny fist and struck his mother in the mouth, knocking out one of her front teeth. This claim to his distinguished future was made when he had been a professional boxer for a year, at a time when it was obvious that he was a young man of considerable promise in the glamorous atmosphere of the prize ring. It is easy to make egoistical claims after the event, but his mother beamingly endorsed the story, after all, she had little to lose and everything to gain by upholding any fantasy her brilliant son might conjure up on the spur of the moment. And, of course, it could have been true, but regardless of this, it can be recorded as one of the many occasions when the self-styled Greatest showed quick wit in gaining publicity for himself.

Long before he was considered as a championship proposition, young Cassius had recognised the essential value of newspapers, radio and television, media that were to gain him a fortune every time he stepped into the ring. It came natural to this negro boy, an impulsive talker, to seize every opportunity to chatter away to reporters and interviewers, especially on his favourite topic—himself, and to provide them with the type of copy he knew would be used. It was not long before boxing writers and sports 'casters sought him out wherever he went because they were certain of getting a good story. Clay never disappointed them, he was an artist at improvisation. He was his own publicity agent, and no one could have done it better.

There is another of those back-dated reminiscences that emphasises his ability—rare for a boxer—to provide a news item that guarantees a quote. At a press conference before an important contest, he told his happily expectant listeners that the first word he uttered as a baby was 'Gee-Gee'. "That's not unusual", said someone. "Most children start by calling a horse that way." "Not in my case", emphatically pronounced Cassius, staring triumphantly at the man who had fallen into the pre-arranged trap. "In my case it meant that some day I would be a Golden Gloves champion", this being the highest honour an American amateur can win; almost a passport into the next United States Olympic Games team.

Of course, this was sheer rubbish, but it got into print and was repeated endlessly on radio and television appearances. Apart from boyhood dreams about emulating such greats as Joe Louis and Sugar Ray Robinson,

9

Young Cassius had little idea about becoming a boxer until he got into his early 'teens. As he eventually reached Golden Gloves status, it was easy to introduce the 'Gee-Gee' baby episode at the appropriate time, thus creating a fictitious prophecy that was in keeping with the natural urge to boast which he was to develop into a fine art. He told everyone in Rome that he would win a gold medal—and did. When becoming a professional boxer he announced to the world that he would win the heavyweight championship of the world and eventually he achieved that high honour. When he was deprived of his title, he solemnly promised to regain it—and did so. A braggart, yes, but efficiently equipped in dedication, skill and thought to realise his prophesies in a way that gripped the imagination of the general public, fight-minded or otherwise, and enable him to claim that he was the greatest of all the heavyweight champions.

Perhaps the most impelling motive in his success was the early realisation that, because of the colour of his skin, he must consider himself as under-privileged; that being a negro meant he could never expect to live on a par with the white people of the world. He resented that mischance of birth from the time he asked his father for the necessary sixty dollars to buy a bicycle. "We ain't got that kind of money", he was told and the irrepressible boy immediately wanted to know why. Taking his brown hand, the parent pointed to it and answered: "That's why, son". It was an acknowledgement that Cassius could not accept and never did, although he did not allow it to build up into a bitter resentment.

Ali has proved himself an accomplished after-dinner speaker, even if he has to be prompted into sitting down on occasions.

He had his own way of overcoming the lowly situation of his existence; to strive to rise, not only above his own race, but to a peak beyond that of any white man. To a boy of mediocre education, Boxing, once it had been brought to his attention, stood out as the surest, if the most hazardous, means of reaching a pinnacle of greatness in human endeavour. It must have given him immense inner satisfaction when white fighters provided stepping-stones to his success, or when he was able to thwart their efforts to win the championship title. Yet, strangely enough, he rarely ridiculed a white rival, confining any pre-fight derision and the practice of talking to an opponent during the rounds, mainly to those of his own race. Maybe the fact that his mother, formerly Odessa Grady, had some Irish blood in her, was responsible for this marked difference.

Environment in the early years has a lot to do with the subsequent moulding of character and career. Cassius Marcellus Clay was born in Louisville in the State of Kentucky. At the time of his birth, on January 17th, 1942, it boasted of 300,000 inhabitants and his arrival was of no significance except to those living in close proximity. His father bore the same three-word name, as had his grandfather and all his male ancestors for six generations, ever since they were slaves on the tobacco plantations of the original Cassius Marcellus Clay who, among other things, had been Abraham Lincoln's ambassador to Russia.

There was no poverty, as such, among the Louisville Clays. Their home was on one floor in a red brick house and young Cassius and his parents, together with a younger brother, Rudolph, shared five rooms. The father, a free-lance sign painter, was proficient enough to keep himself well-employed and his family in more than the bare necessities of life. His income was sufficient for his sons to be provided with a little pocket money and they had no need to take morning or evening jobs during their schooldays as did so many of the coloured boys in the city.

By the age of twelve, Cassius had acquired the much-desired bicycle and boisterously rode its shining frame along the streets in his neighbourhood, waving to passers-by, shouting at his acquaintances, doing everything he could to draw attention to himself. The supreme exhibitionist, putting himself on parade at all times, was life itself and even if youngsters of his own age termed him 'lippy' and adults said he was loud-mouthed, sassy and arrogant, such words of condemnation were music to his ears. He had at that early age all the signs that he might one day become a great actor, a political agitator, or a notability in some form of public enterprise. Yet it was the theft of his treasured bicycle that was to turn his thoughts towards the Fight Game.

Bursting into the local police station, he bawled tearfully that his machine had been stolen. It was natural that he should expect the entire force to turn out and search unstintingly for his lost possession and find the culprit so that he could be adequately dealt with by the owner. "What do you aim to do?" asked Patrolman Joe Martin, who was amused at the coloured lad's vehemence. "I'll whup him up badly", came the reply. "Not only for stealing a bicycle, but for taking mine." Already he was convincing himself that he was in a class above the average.

The policeman was impressed by the boy's sincerity. "If you feel like that", he said "You should learn how to do it." He took Cassius to the city gymnasium where the youngsters of Louisville were taught Boxing and other sports to keep them off the streets. Young Clay stared open-mouthed at two boys who were sparring in the ring, requested that he might have a go and proceeded to pick up the rudiments of the Noble Art in a remarkably short space of time. Unlike the majority of novices, he did not wade in, irregardless of defence, to punch away wildly at his opponent. Instead, he speedily adopted a style of his own, the use of the outer perimeter of the ring for points-scoring and punch-evasion, and an almost unheard of ability to remain on the ropes bent solely on defence, while letting his rival wear himself out in an abortive attempt to land a decisive blow.

With experience, Clay's unique and revolutionary manner of fighting was brought to such perfection that he could break Boxing's golden rule with impunity and waltz round the ring, his arms hanging limply at his sides, his gloves on a level with his hips, defying an opponent to toss a punch in his direction. These tantalising, unnerving and thoroughly unorthodox tactics were extremely dangerous and once or twice he ran into trouble as a result. But superb physical condition and supreme confidence always enabled him to avoid the indignity of an inside-the-distance defeat, while his amazing victories when past his peak were proof that his seemingly precarious ring behaviour had tremendous thought behind it.

Clay's amateur progress was fast and impressive. In the process he had to endure four hard, but to him enjoyable, years as he went through a repetitive training routine, was taught calisthenics appertaining to body building and the rhythm necessary for a boxer; the art of footwork; ringcraft; and the development of a wide repertoire of punches, both in attack and defence. There were, after a time, opportunities in inter-club tournaments for him to exhibit his prowess and learn from experience, and on these occasions Cassius was in his supreme element, glorying in the roar of the crowd, the arclights, and the attention drawn to himself when introduced before the start of a bout.

At the age of 16, Clay had developed into a class amateur and put his foot firmly on the ladder to fame when he won the Kentucky Golden Gloves championship at middleweight. In all he won six State titles and in 1960 became National American Athletic Union champion in the light-heavyweight class. He also won the National Golden Gloves heavyweight championship, although he scaled only 12 st. 8 lbs. (176 lbs.). There was only one other honour he could win as an unpaid boxer and that was an Olympic Gold Medal, the highest glory an amateur can reach. But with natural impetuosity and the keen desire to gain money, he told his friend and trainer that he had decided to become a professional.

Joe Martin explained why this would be a false move. "In boxing an Olympic champion is as good as the No. 10 ranked pro. Win a gold medal at Rome and your earning capacity will be off to a good start.

The heavyweight champion with his parents. Father Cassius and mother, Odessa. Taken at the time of his return contest with Sonny Liston (1965).

And think of the world-wide publicity you will receive." That last remark was sufficient, Cassius was chosen for the Olympic trials at San Francisco, but was only too eager to back out when he realised that he would be flown there. For some reason, quite foreign to his normal self-assurance and bombasity, he was terrified of flying and made an exhibition of himself in the plane, crouching down in his seat, his eyes tightly closed whilst he prayed audibly.

Once on firm land he recovered his usual flamboyancy instantly, defeated the other competitors in his weight division and was an automatic selection for the American Olympic team. But he tore up his return air

13

ticket and borrowed the rail fare back to Louisville rather than face another flight. It was only a temporary escape, however, for the U.S. contingent for Rome journeyed by charter plane and Clay had to summon up all his nervous strength to make the trip. "It was the biggest gamble of my life", he told me afterwards. "But it came off", I said. "I knew it would", he replied immodestly, "But I had to get there and back safely."

The grandeur of Rome sent the young negro into transports of delight. He swaggered about telling all and sundry that he was a certainty for winning gold, his eager face, shining with confidence, denoting his superb physical condition. Within a day or two everyone in the Olympic Village had seen or heard about the coloured youngster from Louisville as he went around snapping photographs, greeting everyone with a flow of eloquence, smiling at the multi-racial competitors, especially the girls. All would have been disappointed had he lost.

He did not lose. In the preliminary round he stopped Y. Becaus of Belgium. In the quarter-finals he accounted for Gennadi Schatkov of Russia. The semi-finals saw him outpoint Tony Madigan from Australia, after a hard battle, and in the final he was confronted by Zbiegniew Pietrzykowski, the Polish representative. Now during Clay's early amateur days, his worst setback in eight defeats out of 108 bouts, was at the southpaw hands of coloured Amos Johnson from Stockton, California, during the Pan-American Games of 1959. Johnson's right hand leading was too much for Cassius, who told himself he would avoid all such unorthodox boxers in future.

Judge his dismay, therefore, when he discovered that the final opponent in his quest for gold was a very efficient southpaw, who had swept aside opposition from another American entry, a German, a Bulgarian and an Italian who happened to be the favourite to win the competition. Three times European champion, Pietrzykowski was a formidable proposition to face and after two rounds it was obvious that Clay would have to do something dramatic in the final three minutes if he was to prove the victor. Cassius was well aware of the situation and came out of his corner determined to get the decision. During the first two rounds he had used the area of the ring to weave and bob defensively, now he launched a devastating assault that left the Pole bloodied and so well-beaten that the verdict in Clay's favour was by unanimous vote and to the satisfaction of the onlookers.

His heart bursting with pride and triumphant pleasure, the 18-year old Cassius stood like a chocolate statue on the medal rostrum to hear the American national anthem played and to have the gold medal hung round his neck. It was the closest he had ever been to the precious metal and he was over-joyed. "I did not take it off for 48 hours", he told me. "I even slept with it." It was pulled out of his shirt and shown to everyone he met. It remains his most treasured possession.

Perhaps as great a moment was the appearance at his hotel the following morning of Floyd Patterson, the current heavyweight champion of the world. Clay's reception of this distinguished visitor was electrifying. He wanted all to know that he

14   (*Right*) The First Touch of Gold. Cassius Clay wearing his medal after winning the Light-heavyweight class in the Rome Olympics 1960. The other boxers are: (2) silver medallist, Zbiegniew Pietrzykowski (Poland); (3) Giulio Saraudi (Italy) and Tony Madigan (Australia).

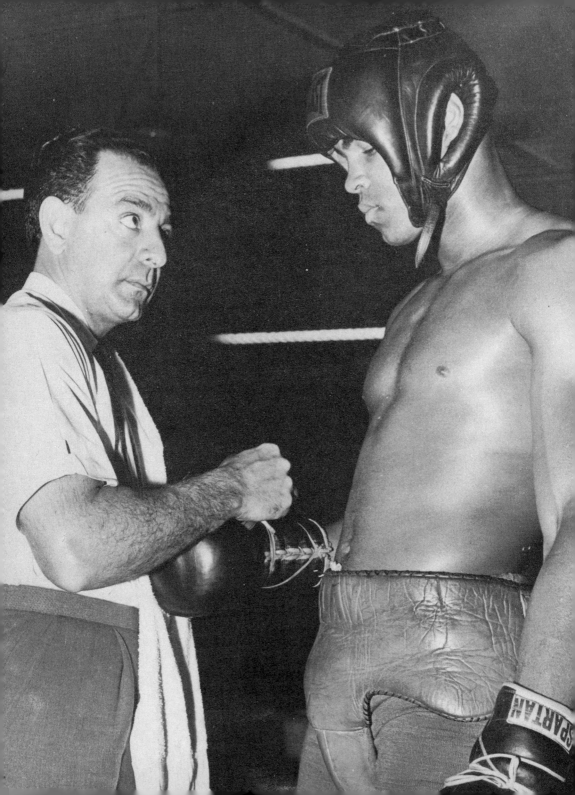

considered the gesture a great privilege, for Patterson was another of his ring heroes. The two coloured champions, one professional, the other amateur, were photographed together, Floyd quiet and modest, Clay noisy and exuberant. They shook hands and Cassius said: "Look after that title. Keep it warm for me in the next two years when I will be ready to take it off you."

When he came off the home-bound plane there was a wide smile across his handsome young features, for flying no longer produced fears. To the assembled pressmen he gave a totally unexpected reply when questioned about turning professional. "I think I would rather be a singer like Elvis Presley", he announced, but when taxed about this astounding statement on his return to Louisville, he replied: "Sure, I want to become a pro, but I did not think it was a good answer to give so soon after the Olympics. They are strictly amateur and I did not want to offend them."

Eleven local businessmen had banded together immediately Clay had been selected to go to Rome. Now they formed a syndicate to sponsor his entry into the paid ranks. All were white, seven were dollar-millionaires. They paid Cassius ten thousand dollars to sign a contract that guaranteed him a salary of 4,000 dollars a year, with all expenses paid, until such time as he might fight for the world title, plus fifty per cent of all his purses up to that point. "You are buying the best there ever was", he told them.

At Clay's request they bought out Patrolman Martin's interest. "He is an amateur", Cassius explained. "He cannot teach me any more now that I am a professional." So they turned their talented investment over to Angelo Dundee, a respected manager and trainer of fighters, whose brother Chris operated a flourishing arena at Miami Beach. Four days after signing with the Louisville financiers, the incorrigible Clay was launched on what was to prove a fantastic career.

(*Left*) Trainer Angelo Dundee was entrusted with the job of improving Clay's style

2. "The Louisville Lip"

They launched him in Louisville, informing the local promoter that he could have Clay for nothing, the Syndicate paying Cassius half of what he would have received if the promoter could have afforded his services. His first opponent was Tunney Hunsaker, a coloured ex-policeman from West Virginia, whose first name should have been an asset in a boxing career. They were matched over six rounds with Clay showing all the faults of a novice professional, but winning handily on points. Trainer Dundee patiently corrected every false move, encouraged him to use his fleet feet with a minimum expenditure of energy, and most important, taught him how to hit with power whilst using every square inch of the ring. But the youngster's rapid development into a star boxer was of his own making. He had so much natural ability, so much imagination, so much variety, that most of his rivals were bewildered into defeat. Dundee's task was one of the simplest because of his pupil's earnest dedication and confident desire to succeed.

Among experienced professionals there are certain routine moves; the left lead, the right cross counter; the jab to the head; the hook under the heart, all coming as a matter of orthodox procedure. Cassius mastered them all, but had his own surprising way of using them. He also employed alarming tactics, such as moving along the ropes, his gloves held at hip level, making an opponent miss by the merest movement of the head; or allowing himself to be pinned in a corner and inviting a rival to belabour his gloves, forearms and broad shoulders.

Dundee spent two further months in tutoring a protege who was fast putting together a style that was to take him to the top in quick time and without defeat. Then he had him performing in the Miami Beach Arena four times within the next 56 days, the Syndicate willingly subsidising the purses. The carefully selected opposition was not of the highest calibre, but it enabled Cassius to fully exploit his natural talents. Local Herb Siler was rescued by the referee in round four; a somewhat flabby Tony Esperti provided Clay with a 19th birthday present by being stopped in round three. Only one round was needed for the referee to intervene on behalf of Jim Robinson from Kansas City, this contest being the main supporting item to a light-heavyweight title bout between coloured Harold Johnson and Jesse Bowdry. Johnson won and afterwards told reporters that he had been aided in his training by having the speedy Clay as a sparring partner.

Angelo persuaded brother Chris that his young fighter was now ready for star billing

18

Ali at work on the platform punch-ball during training

and in his fifth paid contest Cassius was opposed by Donnie Fleeman, a tough Texan heavy, in the main event. They were rewarded with a near capacity crowd of 2,076 fans, who saw stouter resistance to Clay than usual. But after allowing his rival to tire himself out in an abortive attempt to land a winning punch, Cassius set up a sustained body attack under which Fleeman wilted and was in such trouble that the Third Man wisely called a halt in round seven. It was time to let his own folk in Louisville see how well he was progressing, but before leaving Florida, Clay took himself off to the Seabreeze Motel at Palm Beach where Ingemar Johansson had set up a training camp in preparation for his

'rubber' match with Floyd Patterson for the world's heavyweight crown. Here Clay offered himself in the minor role of sparmate and was granted two rounds with the former world champion.

In spite of his unbounded confidence that one day he would reach world championship status, Cassius did not intend to miss any opportunity that might present itself in the furtherance of his high ambitions. When I remarked that by rubbing shoulders with the top fighters, some of their gold might rub off on to himself, the youthful giant—he now stood 6 ft. 3 in. and weighed 195 lbs. (almost 14 st.), with a reach of 77 inches—explained that my reasoning was in error. "These guys might be around when

19

I'm ready to take the championship", he said. "By boxing with them now, I can learn how to beat them later." I asked Johansson what he thought of Clay and he remarked: "He's faster than Patterson and is an extremely good boxer. He jumps around a lot, but is hard to hit. We will be hearing a lot about him before long", he added impressively.

Back in Louisville there was plenty of excitement when it was announced that brash young Cassius was to appear top-of-the-bill at the local arena against Lamar Clark, a white heavy from Utah. This was a step up in opposition, for Clark was more experienced and had a long run of 44 inside-the-distance wins to his credit. Of late, however, he had twice been stopped, but in spite of this, he was the most dangerous and hardest-hitting rival Cassius had been called upon to face so far. When he arrived in Louisville Clark told the local boxing scribes that he regarded Clay as a nobody. "As a matter of fact", he added. "I had never heard of him before I got the contract." He could not have said anything more likely to infuriate Cassius, who considered he had been insulted. "For that remark I shall finish the contest in round three", he threatened. It was the start of a regular prophesy of fight endings that was to gain him added fame. But it also brought Cassius close to disaster. The master in the first round, he had to coast through the next in order to make certain of his boast. In a moment of relaxed concentration, he gave Clark an opening for a heavy right to the chin that shook up the recipient, followed by another that Clay kept away from his jaw, but took in the chest, nearly collapsing a lung.

The largest crowd seen in the Kingdom Hall for two years, totalling 5,441, were brought to a high pitch of excitement as the local boxer reeled back into the ropes, obviously in distress. Many of them had come hoping to see the cheeky Clay receive his come-uppance and at that moment it seemed likely. But they did not know their Cassius. As Clark charged in for the 'kill' he was met by a swift right-hander to the chin that sent him sprawling. There was no chance that he would beat the count and Clay had scored his first clean-cut knockout victory in the fighting time of 4 min. 27 sec. The fans filed out considerably impressed, while in the dressing-room Cassius explained that he had brought Clark's demise forward a round as a reprisal for taking a liberty. Years later he told me that the punch to the chest he had taken from Clark was the hardest he had ever felt.

On the same programme a young coloured heavy was making his pro debut. It was the local boxer Jimmy Ellis, the man who was to become Clay's chief sparring-partner and assume the championship when Cassius was made to forfeit his title through his refusal to be inducted into the U.S. Army six years later.

The win over Clark had proved that he possessed a knockdown punch and the ability to put it into execution. In his next contest, staged in the Nevada gambling city of Las Vegas, he was to demonstrate that he also possessed staying qualities. Opposed to Kolo (Duke) Sabedong, a 6 ft. 6 in. heavyweight from Hawaii, who at 226 pounds outweighed him by 32 lbs., Cassius had to travel the full scheduled distance of ten rounds before gaining a unanimous verdict.

The same thing happened a month later back in Louisville when Alonzo Johnson from Mississippi was still on his feet at the final bell, although well-beaten and out-pointed. Here it must be stated that he failed to forecast correctly the results of his fights with Sabedong and Johnson, both of whom he intended to stop, but found too hard to destroy inside the scheduled distance. But he was back in prophetic form in his next nine contests, all of which ended as he had promised, either during his training or at the weigh-in ceremony, a number of his predictions coming via radio or in television interviews, so that they were widespread to the nation. The bout with Johnson was Clay's first appearance on television, a medium he was to conquer as no other celebrity in any branch of sport or entertainment had done, with audiences of many millions in the days to come. He next faced Alex Miteff, a veteran Argentine heavy, who was stopped in 45 seconds of round six after taking a Clay right-hander to the chin that left him helpless—"The hardest punch I have struck so far", Cassius told reporters afterwards.

Now came Willi Besmanoff, a tough German of ten-years experience, who had been boxing in American rings for five years during which he had met all the leading heavies including the redoubtable Sonny Liston. Besmanoff had stopped Miteff in a single round, but he did not stand a chance against Clay, being jabbed with long lefts and shaken by long-range rights until his whole resistance had gone, whereupon Cassius put him down in the seventh round and then proceeded to batter him methodically until the referee intervened.

Clay had now won his first ten professional bouts in a row, but he was not at all satisfied. At the first opportunity he told the press: "I am tired of fighting unrated bums. I will never get a title shot by knocking out a bunch of has-beens, novices and those who have gone over the hill. The public expects more of me and it is time I received the recognition I deserve and obtain matches against rated heavyweights."

He went further than this when he was a guest at the annual Boxing Writers' Dinner in New York. Asked to say a few words, he did so at length and in a manner that held his listeners spellbound. But it was not merely egotistical eloquence. He was in deadly earnest as he told them a story. "I was down home when I came across a youngster in a gym working out on a heavy bag. He was planning to become a pro fighter. He lived for Boxing and knew all about the most important champions—Joe Louis, Jack Dempsey, Gene Tunney. You know what he said when I asked him what he thought about Floyd Patterson? He asked: 'Who is he?' That's what's wrong with boxing today. It needs a fighting champion, a man who will risk his title against all comers—a champion who will fight *ME*. Like any idol in any sport, the top man owes a debt he must pay. He has no private life and, in the case of a fighter, he must maintain interest in Boxing. You don't do that by fighting once a year and picking your challengers. He must take on anyone who has the courage to meet him. When he walks down the street he must draw crowds; everyone should know him and respect him, he should be the idol of every youngster in the world. If the heavyweight champion is popular, colourful and exciting in the ring, the rest of Boxing will benefit."

Prophetic words, based on the way Cassius conducted himself, not only when he became champion, but on his way up the ladder of fistic fame. Already the fight fraternity was beginning to realise that the voluble coloured boy from Kentucky talked a lot of common sense. Although they named him 'The Louisville Lip', they were always ready, not only to listen, but to quote him.

His self-publicity efforts gained the desired effect. He had now broken into the ratings, being placed ninth behind Sonny Liston, Eddie Machen, Zora Folley, Alejandro Lavorante, Robert Cleroux (Canada), Ingemar Johansson, Cleveland Williams and Henry Cooper. Now he pestered his manager to take each one in turn. The matchmaker at Madison Square Garden sought Clay's services and for the first time his patronising syndicate were able to earn from their pugilistic investment. The selected opponent for his New York debut was Lucien (Sonny) Banks, a coloured fighter from Detroit, about whom not a lot was known around Broadway. Cassius had never heard of him, yet volunteered the information that his rival would go in four.

This forecast, along with Clay's reputation, appeared to be blown skyhigh midway through the first round when the 191¾ lbs. Banks clipped the Louisville lad's chin with a neatly-placed left hook to sit him on his pants on the canvas. Clay seemed more surprised than hurt and scrambled up at 'two'. Being forced to take a mandatory count of eight seconds did not please Cassius, who set about Sonny in over-whelming manner. From then on it was no contest. The speedy Clay had too much of everything for the bewildered Detroiter, who was put down in the second round, badly battered in the third, and was reeling groggily against the ropes after 28 seconds of prophetic round four when Referee Ruby Goldstein called a halt.

Dundee brought Clay back to Miami for his next bout, a ten rounds contest with Don Warner from Philadelphia. In spite of what Cassius had stated in New York, he was still being brought up on un-ranked fighters, and here was a man who had been stopped twice in his last three outings. According to Clay his number was to be up in round four—"One to size him up; two to work him over, and one to finish him off." It all happened as prophesied with Clay causing the referee's intervention after dropping his opponent with a lightning-like right-hander to the chin.

Two months later Dundee transported his fighter across the continent to Los Angeles to meet his first rated opponent, George Logan from Boise in Idaho. They could have brought Logan to Louisville or Miami or anywhere East, but Clay had a special reason for wanting to fight in California. His boyhood idol, Joe Louis, long since retired, was having trouble meeting his income tax demands and had been appointed matchmaker to a promoting syndicate calling themselves United World Enterprises and using the local Sports Arena. Cassius was eager to help the famous Brown Bomber and persuaded his mentors to offer his services, intimating that his presence would be the best means of giving the new venture a successful start. It was agreed and the promoters were rewarded with a crowd of 8,504 who contributed 41,165 dollars, this giving an idea of Clay's fast growing drawing power, for no one in Los Angeles had seen him before, although a great deal had been heard and read about him.

Logan was marked down for four rounds and it was no surprise that this was the precise ending of the contest. Beforehand someone had suggested that as this was Clay's 13th pro bout, it might prove unlucky. "Yes, for George", snapped back the verbose youngster, and after outboxing his sturdy rival for three rounds, Clay opened out to such purpose that the referee's intervention was necessary midway through the next.

All this time Cassius remained in the family home at Louisville, making a daily visit to the gymnasium, religiously going through a meticulous training grind, putting in his daily roadwork. He took every opportunity to appear in public, never failing to attend boxing shows whenever he could get to them, for these provided the atmosphere that best suited his love of the limelight; where he could jolly his way around the ringside, be introduced prior to the main event, visit the dressing-rooms and chat up the working press. He was happiest in such surroundings, although of course, right in his element when he was the star attraction and could display his boxing genius before a packed, yelling multitude. Already he was telling interviewers that he was 'The Greatest'. "The rest are just bums and men like Patterson, Liston and the others are just keeping the Fight Game going until I take over."

New York beckoned again, Clay being selected to meet Billy Daniels, from Brooklyn's coloured quarter. Daniels was unbeaten in his fourteen pro appearances to that date. Almost as big as Cassius, he had no fears about the Louisville man's reputation, even when Clay, carefully sizing up the situation, decided that his rival might last into round seven. He was justified in his shrewdness because Daniels gave him a lot stiffer opposition than the critics suggested, in fact, Clay's performance was disappointing, even if the bout ended as he had forecast, but this time due to the decision of the ringside doctor, who advised against Daniels continuing because of a badly injured left eye that had been cut as early as the second round.

The occasion was one of historic interest, the contest being the last to take place at the St. Nicholas Arena, an ancient edifice in West 66th Street that had begun life in the mid-90s as a skating rink, but which, for the last fifty years, had been a boxing nursery for Madison Square Garden and other big fight venues. Now it was to be demolished to make way for a modern 40-storied block of offices and studios to be erected for the American Broadcasting Company. Naturally, Cassius considered it only right and proper that he should be in at the death. Remembering what had happened on his last New York appearance when he had suffered the indignity of being put on the canvas, Clay boxed very cautiously in the first round, but opened out in the second, a long raking right slicing open a gash over the Brooklyn fighter's left eye. This bled profusely, giving Cassius a target for the night and he popped away at the wound with such effect that the doctor in attendance made frequent visits to the injured boxer's corner.

Despite this handicap, Daniels counter-punched well, tossing over long rights to the head, twice shaking up his rival, but Clay attacked persistently from long range, occasionally darting in to score with swift two-fisted combinations and was well ahead when the doctor signalled to Referee Mark Conn to call a halt as Billy's eye wound had worsened considerably and he had to be saved from serious injury. As it was, ten stitches were necessary afterwards. For once, Clay did not receive acclamation for his victory, indeed, one critic wrote: "If Cassius Marcellus Clay could fight as well as he can talk, he'd be the best heavyweight in the world. Fortunately for Floyd Patterson, however, the cocky 20-year-old Louis-villian's fistic qualifications are considerably short of his eloquent oratorical attainments, and it will be at least another year before he progresses sufficiently to the stage where he can be accepted as a serious threat to the world title."

It must have been an off-night for Cassius because he was back to his true form, both in fighting and prophesying, when he paid another visit to Los Angeles where he was contracted to meet Alejandro Lavorante, a 6 ft. 3½ ins. Argentinian heavy, who had experienced a most successful run until being stopped in ten rounds by Archie Moore in the self-same Sports Arena in which he was due to meet Clay. On that occasion Lavorante, after being heavily pounded about the body, was put down with a powerful left hook, a Moore special, and was so utterly beaten that the referee would not allow the bout to be continued. It was found impossible to restore the limp

South American to a fit state to leave the ring and he had to be taken to the dressing-room on a stretcher, where he remained for an hour before being allowed to go to his hotel. Could such a seriously injured boxer be considered to have recovered sufficiently to make a fit opponent for the up-and-coming Clay within four months of having sustained such a sound beating? No doubt those behind Cassius were satisfied at the choice and Clay himself announced that what Moore had done in ten, he could achieve in five, reasoning that he was twice as good as Ancient Archie.

The fight ended as forecast, Clay using his speed to befuddle the South American. His left jab darted into the bigger man's face like a serpent's tongue, opening a slight cut over Lavorante's left eye as early as the first round. Cassius was moving swiftly and with confident assurance and the Argentinian Giant did not know how to handle him. The second round was following the same pattern when Clay landed flush with a right hand lead to the jaw. Lavorante staggered half-way across the ring into the ropes from the impact and was shaken some more as Clay followed up with a sharp one-two to the chin, the bell sounding before he could inflict further damage.

Lavorante came out swinging in the third, but was too tense and missed badly as Clay glided out of range and countered sweetly. He could have finished the fight in either the third or the fourth round, but played a waiting game, letting his opponent do the leading, whilst he blocked or slipped the punches, being content to jab to the head while he circled the outer perimeter of the ring. Then in the fifth, it happened as predicted. Slow to pull away from a jab, Lavorante was caught by a right to the side of his head that Cassius sent over as quick as a cat dabbing at a mouse. It was by no means a mighty blow, but it was precise and deadly. The South American's knees caved in, he toppled over on his left side and Clay danced a jog as he went over to a neutral corner, then darted back to where Referee Tommy Hart was calling the count over the fallen fighter.

The Third Man chased Cassius back to the corner and Lavorante stumbled to his feet at 'nine'. He had barely raised his gloves before Clay struck with another right to the head, followed by two swift jabs, then a jolting left hook that could not have travelled more than eight inches. Down went the Argentinian on his back, his head bouncing off the bottom strand. The referee did not bother to count, he could see it was all over, the round having lasted 1 min. 48 secs. Clay's triumph was regarded as a major victory, but in retrospect, the opposition had been a great deal less than had appeared on paper. Two months later Lavorante was once more battered into a helpless state, being again taken from the ring unconscious. He remained in a coma for nineteen months before dying at the age of 28.

3. The Greatest

The win over Lavorante made it obvious that Clay's next opponent should be Archie Moore, a man who was boxing professionally before Cassius was born; a cagey old campaigner of nearly 46 (49—if you believed his mother). A man of world-wide experience who, in theory, had been managing his own fistic affairs for most of his long career. Naturally, the pressmen who crowded into Clay's dressing-room at Los Angeles were anxious to know what Fate had in store for the veteran should they meet. "It will have to be four, because it rhymes with Moore", frankly stated Cassius to his avid listeners, and added: "I have told you already that I am the Greatest, now I am the Double Greatest", "How come?" someone asked and Cassius replied: "It took Moore ten rounds to lick Lavorante; I have done it in five, so I must be twice as good as Archie. Yes, sirs, you can write it in your columns that I will demolish Moore in four."

Moore, who himself had never been at a loss for words, was quite calm when Clay's ominous prediction was conveyed to him. "Don't give a boy a man's job" he said, and added: "Despite his incessant chatter that I am an old man and 'washed up', I am not angry with Cassius. Matter of fact, I am very glad that he has such lusty vocal cords.

This boy has talked up such a storm that this match is taking on all the aspects of a 'grudge fight'. That is the best sort of publicity because it sells tickets. He can go on saying what he likes about me so long as it brings the dollars into the box-office. Did he, by the way, tell you that in his early days I gave him a lot of boxing tips? Ask him, he can't deny it. Now I am prepared to give him a real lesson in the Noble Art. I plan to knock his head off, if I can, but it will be an impersonal thing. After all, he is helping me to make a lot of money. Have I any special plans for him. Well, I am perfecting a punch which I call the 'lip-buttoner', and Clay will be the first to see it. It will be the perfect answer to the Louisville Loudmouth. I trust it will make him observe a thirty-day silence."

Right until the time he climbed into the Los Angeles ring Clay kept up an eloquent flow, silencing his press audience at his training camp before imparting some prophetic doggerel lines. "I have left jabs that fire like pistons and are twice as fast as Sonny Liston's. The people cry—'Stop the fight, before Clay puts out his light.' He was trying to remain the great Mr. Moore, for he knew that Clay had predicted 'four'. I swept the old man clean out of the ring, for a good new broom sweeps up every-

26

thing. Some say the greatest was Sugar Ray, but they have not yet seen Cassius Clay." He went on non-stop. "Every 25 years there arises an immortal among heavyweights. The records salute John L. Sullivan, Jack Dempsey, Joe Louis. And now history awaits the arrival of Cassius Clay to fulfil the destiny of greatness."

Quite obviously he believed sincerely in every word he uttered; confidence oozed out of him and the boxing writers went away with filled notebooks, firmly convinced that he would win. They made him favourite at two to one, although none of them expected him to live up to his early win prophesy.

Cassius got a few boos as he entered his corner, whereas Moore received sustained cheers from all parts of the arena. At 212 lbs. (14 st. 8 lbs.) Cassius was the heavier by seven pounds, but a lot of the veteran's poundage was superfluity, in fact, he looked flabby against the youthful muscularity of his athletically-built rival. Whilst extreme confidence beamed from Clay's handsome face, Moore looked dejected and very, very old. Immediately he adopted a crouch, his big arms held protectively in front of his face, while Clay darted round on his toes pecking at this bony barrier, darting a jab to the body, cuffing Archie about the ears. Moore did manage to land one or two good punches in this opening, feeling-out, round, but had to take twice as many from his speedy rival, whose left was like a whiplash.

Accurate jabs beat a tattoo on the older man as Clay moved in and out on gliding feet, while Moore's efforts to counter seemed ponderous in comparison. When the bell sounded Archie seemed resigned to his fate. He was cautioned for a low blow early in the second round, but Clay merely grunted, then launched a brisk attack with a dazzling array of punches, hitting so speedily that Moore did not have a chance to retaliate. Clay was picking up the points without doing a great deal of damage, but in the third round he stepped up the pace, forcing Moore to retreat round the ring under a two-fisted barrage that had him all at sea. Suddenly he left an opening and Clay banged over a right that bounced off the veteran's chin and shook him down to his ankles. Another right on the same target caused Archie's knees to buckle and everyone could see that the end was not far off. Clay could have finished it there and then, but he had ear-marked the fight to end in the fourth, so Moore was allowed to stay until the bell.

It was all over in 95 seconds. Wasting no time, Clay set about his rival with savagery and intent, pounding in punches from both hands, smashing down the last vestiges of Moore's collapsing defence until a thudding left hook to the jaw, and a swiftly following right to the head, deposited the older man on the canvas in an untidy heap. The 16,200 spectators in the Sports Arena rose to their feet and roared with excitement as they saw Clay's prophecy about to be brought to realisation. Moore managed to get to his feet at 'eight', with the impetuous Cassius dancing around within range instead of going to a neutral corner. Then, as soon as Referee Tommy Hart motioned the fight to continue, Cassius put in another dynamic flurry of punches that ended with a right hook to the chin and Archie sank to the canvas for the second time. Again he took

First major victory. The defeat of
Ancient Archie Moore at Los Angeles
in 1962. The referee holds Clay's arm
aloft in round four.

eight seconds in which to rise, but the
writing was on the wall and Clay came in
for the 'kill'. A few fast taps at Moore's
defending arms, a feint to the body, then a
swift right to the temple and down went
Moore again, crumpling to his haunches.
There were no more counts. The Third
Man could see that Archie was hopelessly
beaten and he signalled that the bout was
over. Clay's leap into the air and race round
the ring told the fans that the fight was over
and that he had been true to his boast, the

referee's action alone saving Moore the
indignity of a knockout defeat.

Clay's dressing-room was like a madhouse
as friends and reporters surged in, among
them Sonny Liston, who forced his way
through the milling assembly to con-
gratulate Cassius on his victory. If he expected any thanks, he was soon disillusioned.
"You are next", Clay told the world
champion. "I will take you in eight rounds."
"You will", growled Liston. "If you stay
eight rounds with me, I'll give you the
title". "Then I am as good as the next
champion", responded Cassius. "I aim to be
world titleholder before I am 21 if every-
body does not start ducking me." Already
he was piling up the publicity for their
inevitable meeting.

As Cassius would have attained his
majority in two months time, there was no
prospect of him winning the championship
by his next birthday, nor was it possible for
him to do so during the following year.
Liston, who had been reigning as heavyweight king for only 51 days, having
knocked out Patterson in the unbelievable
time of 2 mins. 6 secs., now had to wait for
his mentors to negotiate terms for the pre-
arranged return contest for the championship. All this took time and ten months
elapsed before Sonny could again demolish
Floyd, this time taking just four seconds
longer. Sonny then set off on a European
tour that lasted many weeks, so that it was
February 25th 1964 before Clay could get
his crack at the world crown, by which time
he was a month past his 22nd birthday.

During this long and impatient waiting
period, Cassius was not allowed to remain
idle. Not that he wanted to be, for he always

28

maintained that the best way to keep fit for fighting was by fighting frequently. Two months after beating Moore, he was in Pittsburg to meet Charlie Powell, a San Diego heavy, whose up-and-down record encouraged Cassius to forecast that he would not stay longer than three rounds. Again he proved that he could conduct a contest to suit his own plans, Powell, a former football player, being counted out after 2 mins. 4 secs. in the prophesied time. For two rounds Clay overwhelmed his rival with a furious onslaught, then went for Powell with renewed fury in the third, two precision-placed left hooks, a right cross, then another left hook to the chin putting the Californian down for good.

Although many followers of sport disliked Clay intensely for his loud-mouthed oratory, a growing number of people respected his logical remarks about Boxing, the way it operated and its legislation in America. An enquiry into professional boxing was being held in Albany by a specially appointed committee, following the death of Benny (Kid) Paret, a Cuban welterweight, in a contest in which he lost his world championship to Emile Griffith. Several prominent boxers, referees and newspaper men were called to the stand to give evidence to the hearing and Clay was one of those invited to add his views. He did so, quietly and gravely, in manner far different from his usual loquacious outbursts whenever he could get more than two people to listen, thus showing that this naturally impetuous young man could discipline himself when occasion demanded.

Rapidly climbing the heavyweight ratings, and now only a place behind Clay in third position, was Doug (Douglas Davis) Jones, born in New York's Harlem five years before Clay emerged in Louisville. For most of his five years as a pro, Jones had been a light-heavyweight, the previous year having lost a close decision to Harold Johnson for the world title. Since then he had stopped Bob Foster and Zora Folley, a rated coloured heavy, and on current form represented the most formidable opponent that Cassius had yet been called upon to meet. That Clay made no effort to avoid a meeting with such a dangerous opponent as Jones when he was already well in line for a title shot, was yet another proof of the great belief Cassius had in his own power and ability.

When it came to calling the round in which Jones would fall, Clay showed that he had some respect for his opponent's class. "Jones likes to mix, so he'll go in six", he said with his now familar poetic predictions. When chided about this he had a second thought and brought the finish down to four rounds. But as soon as he had uttered the words, another rhyme sparked from his fertile brain: "If the sky is blue, he'll fall in two", then added quickly. "Scratch that one the round is still four and if he beats me I'll crawl across the ring and kiss his boots, then leave the country." Many of the critics regarded this as a low estimate. But no one thought of asking Jones for an opinion, who was quietly determined to put the first blot on Clay's so far unblemished professional record.

Whether the paying public thought so or if they were attracted by Clay's magnetic personality, they were intrigued by this contest to such an extent that Madison

29

Square Garden, the mecca for all aspiring fighters, but which had been suffering a lean time of late, enjoyed its fullest attendance for years, a near capacity crowd of 18,732 fans eagerly paying 104,943 dollars, with another 240,000 dollars coming in from theatre-television receipts. Harry Markson, the current Garden boxing director, had to pinch himself to make sure he was not dreaming. "This is incredible", he stated. "For the first time in the Garden's 38-year history, we are sold out days in advance." It was a field day for the ticket spivs who were selling twelve-dollar tickets outside the arena for as much as a hundred-dollars each. The fight was billed as an eliminator for the world title.

On the day of the contest Clay was up early to walk the two blocks from his hotel to the Garden where he stood outside for a few moments gazing at the advertising sign that read: "Boxing—Clay *v* Jones". Apparently satisfied, he went back to his breakfast and was his usual bubbly self by the time he was due to go to the Boxing Commission's offices for the official weighing-in ceremony. There was a great roar of laughter as he burst into the room and stood on the scales, for across his mouth was a 2-inch wide strip of adhesive tape that effectively sealed him into silence for the first time in his life. But he tore it off as soon as the reporters clustered round for a quote. They were not disappointed, for he spouted a poem that he said he had composed during the night:

My secret is self-confidence,
A champion at birth.
I'm lyrical, I'm fresh, I'm smart,
My fists have proved their worth.

Marcellus vanquished Carthage,
Cassius laid Caesar low,
And Clay will flatten Douglas Jones
With a mighty, measured blow.

Weighing-in at 202½ lbs., Clay had an advantage of over a stone. He was taller and possessed a longer reach, but Jones was un-ruffled. Indeed, he very nearly brought off a sensational win when he set up a strong attack in the opening round, catching up with the fast-pedalling Cassius and nailing him with two solid rights to the head, plus a stinging left hook to the chin that sent the Louisville Lip bouncing back into the ropes. The fans thundered at this unexpected sight, for it was obvious that Clay had been shaken. He sagged into the hemp in a half crouch, his seat well over the bottom strand, his chin tucked in, his gloves held high. In a matter of seconds his confident poise had vanished—now he was suddenly defending his fistic life. Yet his recovery was equally quick. Jones was allowed to hammer in what were intended to be finishing punches, but which Cassius absorbed on his arms and shoulders, then he slipped away out of trouble to pepper his advancing opponent from long range.

In the second and third rounds the Harlem man maintained his aggression, pressing his rival into retreat, striving to put over another deadly right hook. But Clay had learned his lesson and kept Doug at distance with some fast jabbing that was amazing from a heavyweight. When they came out for the fourth round there was a distinct air of expectancy from the onlookers, but very soon it was apparent that Cassius was not to be allowed to keep up with his forecast. As

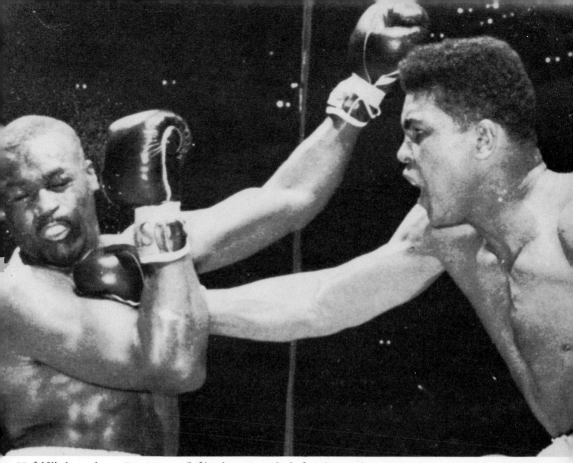

Unfulfilled prophecy. Doug Jones (left) who upset Clay's fourth round prediction by staying the distance of ten rounds in New York in 1963.

Jones remained determined and aggressive and Clay kept trying abortively to catch him with a telling punch, so the fans began to boo louder and louder until, at the end of the round, the building shook with the noise. From that moment, no matter what Cassius did, he was booed for it, the demonstration continuing against him until the final bell. The taunting went on even when Clay got in damaging blows that staggered his rival, but the fact that he was unable to score a knockdown went against him and Jones was cheered as he attacked stolidly and received a great roar when he was still on his feet at the final bell, having survived a great two-fisted burst from Cassius that came just before the finish.

The unanimous points verdict in favour

of Clay was badly received. There were loud catcalls when it was announced that Judges Artie Aidala and Frank Vorbes both cast 5–4–1 in favour of Cassius, and there was a stormy outburst when it was revealed that Referee Joe Loscalzo voted it 8–1–1, a score that seemed ridiculous and which evoked loud cries of 'Fix' and 'Fake'. Was it a bad verdict? I do not think so. In my view the judges were about right. They awarded the first four rounds to Jones, considered the next round even and gave the last half of the contest to Clay who landed the most scoring punches. But he had had to put in a desperate rally to gain the decision. A poll was taken among the ringside pressmen which resulted in twelve of them voting for Jones, nine for Clay, while two thought the contest had been drawn.

Afterwards, most of the boxing writers crammed into Clay's dressing-room. For a few minutes he was in a strangely subdued mood, having left the ring to sustained booing, leaving Jones to acknowledge the whole-hearted applause. But it did not take long for Cassius to recover his natural brashness. He was in no way dismayed at the result. "Jones tricked me by going the full ten", he admitted. "I'm giving up predicting the round in which I will win. It's too much of a strain. People are so hypocritical. They came to see me whipped. They hated me for winning. I hit Jones with twice as many punches as he landed on me. That's why they were upset. The referee's score was the most accurate of the three officials. Look at my face. I'm unmarked. I'm as pretty as a girl." Several years later Cassius watched the film of the Jones fight

with his first wife. At the end his new bride remarked: "I thought Jones beat you, honey", to which Clay replied: "Yes, it sure looked that way."

Jones' comment was characteristically brief: "I don't think much of him", he said. "He never hurt me. I don't think he's very good." Champion Sonny Liston was equally terse: "I'll take him in no more than three rounds. He don't even know how to stop a punch or how to run and I will catch him early. But I'll get locked up for murder if we're ever matched."

Jack Solomons, the London promoter, had flown over specially to see the contest, having in his pocket a contract for Clay to meet Henry Cooper, the British champion. He was undismayed at the news that Cassius would be picking up over £32,000 for the Jones fight, and was smiling happily after a conversation with William Faversham, one of Clay's syndicate backers. There was talk of a return bout with Jones, but Cassius did not see the sense in this, their bout having been billed as an eliminator. With no prospect of a title match with Liston, it was decided to accept Solomon's offer of £25,000, plus travelling expenses, and take on Cooper, whose record against American fighters did not suggest that he would be too troublesome.

The fight with Cooper was fixed for June 18th at Wembley Stadium. Clay arrived three weeks beforehand with an entourage of a dozen, including his brother Rudy, his trainer, Angelo Dundee, a 'bodyguard', and two sparring partners, former opponent Don Warner and the aforementioned James Ellis, both of whom were to have minor contests on the same pro-

In the gymnasium with his former sparring-partner, Jimmy Ellis (right) who later fought Ali but was stopped in 12 rounds.

gramme. As usual, Clay seized every opportunity to gain publicity from the moment he landed. When asked at the customs if he had anything to declare, he said: "Plenty. I am the greatest boxer of all time and I am the prettiest. I will stop Cooper in five rounds, but don't bank on it, I might finish it in the first, so come early." At a reception given by the promoter at Isow's Restaurant in Soho, he was in his element. Both boxers were asked to speak, but whereas Cooper hoped for a good fight, Clay went on talking about himself and what he intended to do until the British champion rolled up a napkin into an ear-trumpet, which brought light relief and showed that Henry was undisturbed at the threat of his promised extinction.

A firm believer in publicity, Ali was styling himself 'The Greatest' back in his earliest Cassius Clay days.

Throughout the intervening time, Clay made appearances at every possible boxing occasion, even travelling to Nottingham to see a fight for a British title. He held up the traffic in Piccadilly Circus and never missed a chance of drawing attention to himself. Even so, he was up every morning at five o'clock to do his roadwork in Hyde Park. At the weighing-in ceremony at the London Palladium, to which the general public was admitted free of charge, Clay took the centre of the stage. At 207 pounds (14 st. 11 lbs.) he had an advantage of 21½ pounds, and certainly looked the bigger of the pair. After the ceremony I followed Cassius out of the theatre and in doing so we passed a door marked 'Prop Room'. At once he darted inside and I followed him. On a table, neatly laid out for that evening's performance of *Kings of Mirth*, featuring The Crazy Gang, were five plush purple velvet, gold and jewel-encrusted crowns. Clay tried each for size and, in spite of my remonstrances, walked out with one perched jauntily on his head, climbed into a waiting car and was off. I thought the last had been seen of it, but I had under-estimated the Kentucky Showman.

When he made the long trek from the dressing-rooms to the centre of the famous football stadium, he was wearing the crown over a white ankle-length dressing-robe that bore on the back 'Cassius Clay—The Greatest'. He was accompanied all the way by catcalls and booing, for his oratorical outbursts in the press had not made him popular with followers of boxing in England, and as he neared the ringside one irate fan took off his shoe and tried to knock the crown from the arrogant wearer's head.

But Clay kept it on until he was in his corner, when an official of the British Boxing Board of Control removed it and, I suppose, it was returned post haste to the West End.

While the gloves were being fastened, Cassius leaned over the ropes and reminded the boxing reporters of his five rounds forecast. Most of them yawned, while the 35,000 crowd who braved a cold and gusty night, and only half-filled the vast arena, booed incessantly, with occasional bursts of cheering for Cooper who was begged to 'knock his block off'. Referee Tommy Little called them to the centre of the ring for the usual instructions, to which Clay paid not the slightest attention, being mainly concerned in eyeing his opponent disdainfully. They returned to their corners, the bell clanged and the contest, advertised as a final eliminator for the world heavyweight title, began.

No doubt bearing in mind his fifth round prophecy, Clay boxed very lethargically in the first two rounds while Cooper, urged on by the roaring fans, did all the attacking, jabbing with the left and crowding in to get in his shorter punches, his famed left hooks whistling dangerously around the ears of the coloured American. When Henry worked his way in and attacked the body, Clay was guilty of holding, for which offence he was reprimanded by the referee, who halted the proceedings to wag a warning finger at Clay. As they resumed, Cooper chased his rival into the ropes where he banged away furiously with both hands. Cassius did not like this burst of belligerence from a man he had so often described as a 'bum'. He was forced to back off and more than once look-

ed at Mr. Little, as if the Britisher was not observing the rules. But everything that Henry was doing was perfectly legal and the only conclusion I could come to, was that Clay was surprised by the show of aggression on the part of his opponent. He looked particularly grieved when coming out of a break, Cooper whipped in a smart punch to the face.

There was terrific cheering for Henry as he returned to his corner at the bell, for it was obvious that he must have taken the major points in that first round. In the second, he again relied on his left, jabbing it out as he went forward, not to keep Clay at bay, because Cassius was quite content to circle the ring, his gloves at his sides, occasionally bringing up a long left to poke Henry's face. There did not seem any power at all behind these lackadaisical thrusts yet soon I observed there was a reddening mark under the Britisher's left eye. Perhaps Henry was aware of it, as was his trainer, Danny Holland, who reached for his cuts kit, for Cooper now increased the pace and intensity of his attack, striving to land a left hook on his elusive foe. He got through with several, but Cassius blocked or avoided most of them, while Henry's attempts to toss a right went hopelessly astray as his rival drew back or swerved to avoid them. Clay was purposely letting the British champion wear himself out in an effort to land a decisive punch and the bell came with the American unmarked, while Cooper was now leaking blood from his cut.

They patched up the wound, but now it was Clay's target for the rest of the contest. He lured his rival into close range then struck with a fine right that turned Henry's

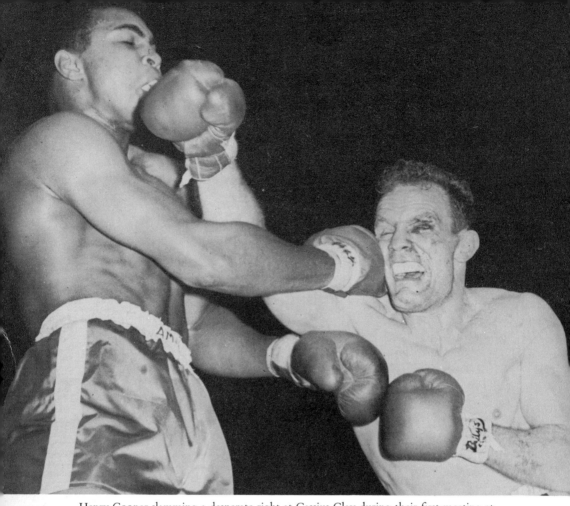

Henry Cooper slamming a desperate right at Cassius Clay during their first meeting at Wembley Stadium. The British champion's damaged left eye caused the bout to be halted in round five.

injury into a gory mess. Feeling the warm blood only inspired Cooper into renewed fury. Tearing into the American, he let fly with both fists, but his aim was understandably erratic and he was unable to break through, while Clay moved nonchalantly round the ring, acting the fool, posing and gesticulating, but now and again getting in

a blow that caused more havoc on Cooper's features. At the end of the round it was generally reckoned that the honours had to go to Henry on sheer aggression in spite of his battered countenance.

It now seemed obvious that Clay was coasting along in readiness to make his prediction come true. Two long-range rights in quick succession split open Cooper's left eyebrow. It oozed blood profusely and it seemed that Henry's defeat was certain because Referee Little was showing concern about the state of his injuries. Clay was still backing off, whipping in a damaging punch every now and then, while Cooper chased him round the ring, lashing out fiercely, fully realising that his time was fast running out. The calm look on Clay's face was in direct contrast with Henry's bloodied visage.

Then it happened! Suddenly Cooper leapt forward, his left arm curved and his famous hook—the punch that the assembled fans had been waiting, even praying for from the start of the contest—landed with devastating effect on Clay's pretty chin and down he went, looking anything but The Greatest as he sprawled ungainly on his back in a neutral corner. And then the loudest roar I have ever heard at a fight arena rent the air. His eyes glazed, his left arm hooked over the second rope, otherwise he must have struck his head against the taut hemp, Cassius sank backwards to the canvas, his mouth agape, a vacant expression on his face, completely oblivious to where he was or what had happened. He got to his hands and knees; blood was trickling from his nose, and he was on the point of rising when the bell clanged to end the round and come to his rescue. At that moment the timekeeper had reached 'four' and was raising his arm for the next beat. Clay had been saved from ignominious defeat by a few seconds.

Many have ventured opinions as to how the fight would have ended had Clay got to his feet. In my view he was in such a groggy state that Cooper, noted for his finishing powers, would have needed to land just one more left hook and the American would have been knocked unconscious and 'out' for good. What effect such a result would have had on the world heavyweight situation has also been argued about. In my opinion—very little! Cooper would probably have got a fight with Liston and even in the event of winning, would have found that his chief challenger was Cassius Clay. Abject defeat would not have demoralised The Greatest, his dedication was so devouring at that stage of his career, that he would have come back triumphantly, as he was to do with such effect so many years later.

Back to Wembley Stadium. During the interval following the fourth round, in which the vast arena rocked with excited cheering, Cooper's handlers worked frantically to stem his wounds and send him out refreshed and eager to finish the job. But in Clay's corner all sorts of things were happening. Suddenly trainer Dundee called over the referee and explained that Clay's left glove had burst, the horsehair stuffing protruding through a long slit. How this freak accident happened has never been explained. Referee Little went to the ringside and spoke to the Board of Control officials seated there. Any replacement for the damaged glove was a quarter-of-a-mile away and a discussion was still going on when the bell sounded for the fifth round and while a cleaned-up Cooper emerged from his corner and strode straight into battle, Clay came out with almost a bare fist showing through his left glove.

It was the moment of truth for Cooper, and Cassius set about the British champion with such ferocity and intent that in a matter of seconds Henry's face was a gory mask again, the blood streaming from his lacerated eyebrow, smothering his chest. Irregardless of this gory spectacle, Clay struck fast with both hands at his half-blinded rival, sending the gallant Cooper staggering under his precision blows, doing a demolition job that had the big crowd suddenly silenced. It could not go on, Cooper's face looked horrible and in 75 seconds it was all over, the referee intervening to send Henry to his corner and raise Clay's arm in token of victory.

Cassius went berserk. While unwarranted boos sounded from the disappointed fans, he ran round the ropes, yelling at the reporters and ringsiders that once again he had carried out his prophesy, although not strictly to the letter. He had said that Cooper would fall in five, but it was he who had fallen, a bare few seconds separating him from defeat. He was whistled at derisively and jeered all the long way back to the dressing-room, while for Cooper the cheers thundered at every step he took. But Cassius could now claim, louder than ever that he was indeed 'The Greatest' and the man whom Sonny Liston, the 'Big Ugly Bear', as Clay called him, would have to face in the next defence of his world crown.

4. Richest Prize in Sport

Heavyweight boxing has had its great moments of thrills, sensational happenings, colourful characters and headlined stories. That is the Fight Game, its unpredictability that makes it so fascinating and spell-binding. In his so far short career Cassius Clay had provided all those ingredients that go to make up this spectacular sport. Now his two championship contests with Sonny Liston were to evoke both surprise and incredibility, even alas, suspicion, although it is only right to say that the young man from Louisville had no part in any machinations or plots that may have been involved. He entered into the first bout, staged under the aegis of his home-town backers at Miami, with his usual brash confidence. To him, it was just another contest, albeit the most important in his three years of ring warfare and the goal at which he had been aiming since boyhood. It meant unbounded riches and above all, the glamorous lime-light of the sporting universe. At no point, I am positive, did he have any hand in planning the outcome of his championship affairs, either as a contender or defender. It would have been completely foreign to his ego and natural honesty.

Whereas Clay was sponsored by business-men of integrity and professional boxing people of long-standing and respect, the same could not be said about those who were suspected of being behind Liston, although there was nothing untoward about Jack Nilon, his manager of record. With his brother, Bob, Nilon had formed Liston into a company entitled 'Inter-Continental Promotions', with Sonny owning $47\frac{1}{2}$ per cent. of the stock. It subsequently came to light that this body paid Clay (before the first fight) fifty thousand dollars for the right to stage a return contest if the title changed hands, an extra-ordinary procedure which was rigorously criticised by the Florida State attorney, Richard Gerstein, at a post-fight enquiry. It was also disclosed that a well-known gambler and bookmaker had enjoyed the full run of Liston's training camp and was present in the champion's dressing-room prior to the start of the championship battle. There was also the fact that Sonny, born at Pine Bluff, Arkansas, had something of a police record. He had even served a nine-month term in prison for assaulting a police officer. He had picked up his boxing whilst in a reform school, being encouraged by the padre, Father Stevens. It was claimed that Liston had left jail a reformed being, but since becoming champion he had been involved in several brushes with justice and appeared to consort with undesirable charac-

One of Ali's seconds wearing a sweater that carries the famous slogan—"Float Like a Butterfly, Sting Like a Bee".

ters rather than more law-abiding citizens.

As usual, ninety per cent of the pre-fight ballyhoo came from Clay. He had named his opponent 'That Big Ugly Bear' and day by day issued threats as to what he intended to do with the champion once they were in the ring together. "Liston is mine, he will fall in nine. If he wants to mix, he will end in six." There was a lot more, with the pugilistic poet barely giving himself time to rhyme or scan. As for Liston, he kept reiterating that it would end in three rounds and he would probably be arrested for murder afterwards. He could say nothing, however, to match Clay's catch phrase—'*I will move like a butterfly, but sting like a bee*', which, after all, was a prophetic utterance, yet denoted the only real way in which he could win the championship. While Clay's ranting against Liston was mainly for publicity purposes and his delight in holding an audience, there was some keen resentment in the fact that Sonny had denied Cassius the opportunity to carry out his intention of becoming world champion before he was twenty-one. The return match with Patterson and Sonny's European tour had been responsible for the upset to Clay's earnest prediction and he held the champion responsible for his failure to make his words come true.

The bookmakers made Clay the underdog in the betting at 7 to 1 against, almost ridiculous odds in a sport in which anything can happen. They based their judgment on comparisons between the records of the two men. Liston had been beaten only once in 35 contests when he lost on points in a contest in which his jaw had been broken as early as round one. But this had been in the very early days of his professional career. Of his wins, 25 had been scored inside-the-distance, seven in the opening round, including his two quick wins over Patterson, from whom he had won the title.

On the other hand, Clay was undefeated in 19 bouts, only four of which had gone the scheduled course. Liston had been a professional for eleven years, two of which had been lost through detention, while Cassius had but three paid years behind him. Sonny, at thirty was the older man by eight

Muhammad puts on a terrified expression as he views the astronomical prices being charged for admission to his heavyweight title challenge to Sonny Liston at Miami in 1964.

Worrying the Big Bear. Two illustrations of the way Clay harassed Sonny Liston at the weigh-in for their title fight. Even when pushed into the background, Cassius continued to hurl insults at the champion.

years and there were marked physical differences that seemed in Liston's favour. His abnormal reach of 84 ins. was two inches more than Clay's, and his chest measurements were two inches extra, both normal and expanded. His $17\frac{1}{2}$ ins. biceps were immense against the challenger's 15 ins., and his mighty fist was $2\frac{1}{2}$ ins. bigger at $15\frac{1}{2}$ ins. Cassius at 6 ft. 3 ins. was the taller of the pair by two clear inches.

If Clay's pre-championship behaviour and publicity tactics had been something new to the Fight Game, his antics at the weighing-in ceremony were fantastically hysterical, even embarrassing. He came bouncing into the room wearing a natty sports outfit and swinging a cane. Emblazoned in red on his navy blue jacket were the words "Bear Huntin' ", denoting that he intended to carry out his threat and tame 'That Big Ugly Bear'. As he approached the waiting officials who surrounded Liston, Clay began to rant and rave at his forthcoming opponent, shouting out what lay in store for Liston, declaring that Cassius Clay was The Greatest and repeating all the jibes and insults that everyone had heard daily for the past month. His voice rose to screaming pitch and his unruliness was such that my nearest neighbour remarked: "If it wasn't Clay, he'd be put in a strait-jacket and carted off." All efforts to quiet him down were of no use and finally Ed Lassman, President of the World Boxing Association, under whose auspices the title contest was to be fought, ordered Clay to be removed to his dressing-room, whereupon it was publicly stated that he had been fined 2,500 dollars (£900) for 'disgraceful conduct', an announcement that was heartily cheered by an assembly who were disgusted that a usually sombre occasion should be turned into a circus act.

All through Clay's unceasing roaring, which continued long after he had been admonished officially, Liston remained dour and taciturn, as if he could not hear what was going on or was merely turning a deaf ear to it all. If it was meant to put Sonny into a state of nervousness or stir him into an emotional retaliation, Clay's tedious tirade failed hopelessly. Perhaps it was intended to boost his own morale, for after medically examining Cassius, Dr. Alexander Robbins, the Florida State Boxing Commission's doctor, told me that the fighter's pulse rate was in excess of 100. "It's as though he is scared to death", he added.

While the paid attendance of 8,927 only half-filled the Convention Hall, millions watched the contest on closed-circuit television throughout the world, the receipts from this source, plus radio and film revenue, amounted to 2,686,000 dollars, of which Liston's 40 per cent share was 720,000 dollars and Clay's 20 per cent, just half that sum. He was in the really big money at last. The contest was scheduled for fifteen rounds, the referee being Barney Felix and the judges were Bill Lovell and Gus Jacobson. They were to use eight-ounce gloves, there would be a mandatory count of eight seconds in the case of a knockdown, but the regulation that three knockdowns in a single round would constitute a knockout defeat was waived for this contest. Almost without exception, the ringside critics tipped Liston to win in a few rounds.

Sonny looked impregnable as he lumbered forth from his corner at the starting bell, while Cassius kept well out of reach and glided, even walked round the ring, his hands hung low, his shoulders moving, his head bobbing, making ground before Liston's advance, yet not seeming to do so. Liston was jabbing with his long left, getting one or two through, but without any jarring effect. Sonny tried hard to pin Cassius in a corner, but the challenger slipped away, although not before he had taken a hard right swing to the body. Clay's dancing feet made his rival miss with his big punches and now Cassius began to counter Liston's leads. He would draw a jab from the champion, dodge it, then come back with a

43

smart left to the face.

Doggedly Sonny came after his challenger, again trying to force him into a corner, in fact, Cassius let Liston think he was going to be trapped, thus bringing the champion into range for some swift and accurate blows from either hand. Sonny had to take several stabs to the forehead that had him pausing, whereupon Clay landed a hard left to the jaw, followed by a right to the head. Liston met Clay's next two-fisted burst with a long left to the jaw and they were mixing it when the bell sounded. Neither of them heard it and continued to swap punches until the referee got between them. It was Clay's round, but that was of little consequence.

Cassius began circling as soon as he left his corner and Liston went in pursuit, landing a light left, but missing with a savage right. The champion scored with a right to the body that made Clay step back into the ropes. As he bounced off he was caught by a left to the head, but it was a light blow. Again Sonny sent his rival on the retreat and did the bulk of the scoring. But there was nothing behind the shots, nor did Clay land anything but light punches and the round went to Liston on aggression, even if it had proved unproductive.

The fans who had been waiting for the fireworks to start, now began to realise that there was not going to be a speedy demoliiton of the challenger. Clay was still back-pedalling and leaning back on the ropes, avoiding most of Sonny's attempts to land a really decisive blow. Cassius kept popping in his counter punches and soon it was observed that Liston was bleeding from the nose, then from a cut under his left eye. Yet he got through with some stiff punches to the body, took a left and a right to the head in return, then came in very determinedly to make play on Clay's mid-section. There was no infighting and Sonny was unable to grab his opponent with one hand and pound him with the other in the way he had pulverised Patterson. The honours of the round again went to the champion.

It was obvious that Liston was concentrating on a body attack, but finding Clay a most elusive target. Sonny got through with a number of swings, but they fell short of being damaging because of Clay's amazing powers of avoidance. Blows that seemed likely to be driven right through his frame were reduced to mere prods and all the while Cassius was putting in the occasional jab or cross, blows that snapped back the champion's head and gave Clay the edge on the round. He was rubbing his eyes with the back of his gloves when he returned to his corner and complained to Angelo Dundee that his eyes were smarting and he could not see. The referee was sent for and a complaint made that a chemical of some sort had been applied to Liston's gloves which had affected the challenger's eyes.

The official went over and examined Sonny's gloves, even smelt them, but no trace of an irritant could be found. Meanwhile, Clay was begging Dundee to take off his gloves; that he could not see properly and did not wish to continue the fight. He was still sitting on his stool when the bell sounded for the fifth round and Barney Felix beckoned him to come out and continue the fight. Afterwards he told me that as Clay was pushed to his feet by his trainer,

Sonny Liston swinging crudely at the 'butterfly' evasiveness of his challenger at Miami in 1964.

he was on the point of stopping the contest and declaring Liston as the winner. Dundee had to give his fighter some stern coaxing. "Go out and take him", he yelled. "This is the big one. The guy is just ready for plucking."

All through the fifth round Clay was in desperate retreat, rolling along the ropes, intercepting blows from Liston with his gloves, arms and elbows. He was still having trouble with his eyes, blinking them as he retreated on dancing feet. When Liston came in, Cassius resorted to holding, but Sonny punched himself free and now the

challenger was subjected to a severe pounding about the body. It was all Liston now, with Clay in a seemingly desperate state and it looked as if, at any moment, the champion would land the pay-off punch. He clipped Clay on the chin and sent him reeling into the ropes, but his follow-up was halted by two lefts to the face, then Clay slipped away and the bell halted hostilities.

What Angelo or anyone else may have said to Cassius in the next interval, I do not know, but whatever it was the result was electrifying. Perhaps they had noted that Liston's legs had gone rubbery; maybe they

A distinct look of apprehension on the face of Liston during the 6th round of the Miami championship fight when Clay was on the attack. Liston retired at the end of the round leaving Cassius a sensational winner.

detected signs of dejection on Sonny's grim features. Anyway, out came Clay as if he had nothing to beat. He was back in his ultra-confident mood once again and hit out at the champion as if he were nothing more than a large punch-bag. Lefts and rights bounced off Sonny's head and soon the champion's nose was bleeding again. All that Liston did in reply to this brisk bombardment was to lunge at Clay's body, but the challenger was not worried by these punches, dangerous as they appeared to be. Cassius absorbed them, nor was he bothered when the champion got in the occasional

long left. His own blows were not ripping Liston apart, but they were point scorers and at the bell he had won the round well.

Midway through the interval Liston's handlers were seen trying to attract the referee's attention and presently Barney Felix went along the ropes from the neutral corner where he had been making up his score-card to see what it was all about. Cassius must have been watching very closely, because as the bell was sounding to start the seventh round, he leapt from his corner and waved his arms about as if the fight was over. It was, but Clay was way

The crowded ring after Clay had been announced as the new world champion. Amidst the turmoil he is telling the fans that he has beaten 'The Big Ugly Bear' as he said he would.

ahead of everyone else in the arena in knowing it. Sonny sat with head bowed while his handlers conveyed to the referee the fact that the champion could not continue; that he had injured his shoulder and was in pain. It was his manager, not Liston, who made this dramatic decision, and while Clay was dashing excitedly about the ring, shouting that he had told them so and had proved himself The Greatest, poor Sonny had to listen to the crowd's loud-spoken disgust at his retirement. They cried 'Fake' and 'Fix' and called him a coward and a quitter. But without any doubt Cassius Clay was the new heavyweight champion of the world and he let everyone in the world know it as he yelled and gesticulated in a state bordering on hysteria, whilst his handlers did their utmost to restrain him. Meanwhile the noise was deafening, no one except Clay being satisfied with the way the championship fight had ended. Fans, officials and press were united in regarding the finish with the utmost suspicion.

"I am the Greatest", the triumphant Clay shouts over and over again as he is embraced by one of his seconds. Trainer Angelo Dundee (on the right) yells exultantly, as well he might, for it was his prompting that won the fight for Cassius.

The Florida State Boxing Commission endorsed public opinion by seizing Liston's purse pending a medical report on Sonny's alleged arm injury, but after the ex-champion had been examined by eight doctors, it was accepted that he was suffering from a torn biceps tendon of sufficient severity to justify his retirement. But this evidence did not satisfy the boxing fraternity who held the long-established view that a champion does not quit in his corner and there was general feeling throughout America that the pre-arranged return title fight between the pair was something to be avoided.

The New York State Boxing Commission banned the bout and urged the World Boxing Association and the World Boxing Council to act likewise; the British Boxing Board of Control also came into line and it appeared that there was no likelihood of another Clay v Liston match. It emerged that while no return fight clause existed in the original contract, Clay was stated by his sponsors to be under a moral obligation to give Liston an opportunity to win back his crown. But after his humiliating defeat, would Sonny be likely to insist? There was also the fact that the U.S. Army was demanding Clay's services for a two-year period, a move that would automatically rule out a second contest. But time heals all wounds, softens anger and dulls memories, while the making of money over-rides all in due course. The new champion went off to tour the coloured African countries, while Liston nursed his wounds, declaring his intention of being Clay's first challenger, and even promised to win back the championship.

5. Muhammad Ali

At what point in his life Cassius Clay decided to adopt the Muslim faith only he can say, but it must have been in his mind for a considerable time and, like everything he did, the public announcement of his acceptance was beautifully timed—after he had become world heavyweight champion, when the impact would be most pronounced. But during his training for Liston he had slipped away from Miami to attend a Muslim meeting in New York, and no doubt he had been in close contact with the leader, Elijah Muhammad, before that. At the outset there may have been some thoughts of the publicity value in joining the movement, but fundamentally Clay was emotionally attracted and his allegiance was fully sincere. Here it is vitally important to stress that he joined a religious body, not a violently aggressive party. He has stressed again and again that he is not a so-called Black Muslim, but a disciple of the true Muslim faith, and there is a vast difference. It is true that at first he was seen in the company of Malcolm X, a well-known racialist, and had started to call himself 'Cassius X'. But as soon as he realised there was a distinction between the two sects, he quickly left the turbulent offshoot movement, and reverted to the more pacific body, changing his name to Muhammad Ali in deference to its leader.

At first the boxing fraternity chose to ignore this change of title, but Ali was insistent, on one occasion refusing to enter the ring at Madison Square Garden to be introduced unless he was announced by his Islamic name. He told the world that his original name denoted slavery, that it had been forced on him, as it had been forced on his father, grandfather and great-grand-father. He took pride in denouncing it. He explained that the true Muslim faith did not permit the use of alcohol or tobacco, the taking of drugs or promiscuous sexuality. He had banned these things from the start of his athletic life, so they came as no hardship. In addition, Muslims did not believe in violence or killing, even in wartime, a factor that was to have a serious and detrimental effect to his future. His whole-hearted adherence to his new religion was also to cause the break-up of his marriage—something that it was in his inborn nature to avoid. When approached to make an Arabic film in Egypt entitled 'Knockout', he stipulated there should not be any scenes showing him kissing, drinking, smoking or engaging in any other activity contrary to Islamic tradition.

After the first almost unanimous outburst against a return fight with Liston which Ali ignored, there began moves to bring this bout to fruition, the best reason being that no one believed the first meeting to have been a true reflection on the abilities of the two men. There was also the fact that there was no other pairing that would be as big a draw. In spite of the W.B.A. ban, the Boston Garden promoters secured the fight and the State of Massachussetts did not seem unduly perturbed when it was outlawed by the Association, nor were Liston and Ali, or their adherents bothered when the title was declared 'vacant'. They went ahead and the contest would have come off on November 16 as planned, but for the champion being rushed to hospital for an immediate hernia operation just three days beforehand, much to the disappointment of the fifteen delegates from the United Nations who had been specially invited by Ali to 'watch for fair play'.

It meant a delay of six months, but Boston retained its hold on the championship contest, whereas the W.B.A. matched Ernie Terrell, a giant from Chicago, with the more experienced Eddie Machen, from Redding, California, labelling the fight as for the world heavyweight crown. Terrell won this all-coloured contest and was duly recognised as Clay's successor in those states that owed allegiance to the W.B.A. Elsewhere, everyone regarded Ali as title-holder and wondered who would be affected most by the long lay-off—champion or challenger.

In the interim, two important things had happened to Muhammad Ali. He had been turned down for military service because he was not up to the minimum mental standards required, although he had passed physically. It was added by Stephen Ailes, U.S. Secretary of the Army at a Congressional Committee, that three psychologists were satisfied that the boxer was doing his best in the mental tests. It was then revealed that while his High School athletic record was high, Ali's academic points were very low as he finished 376th in a total of 391. The other main event after winning the title was his marriage to 24-year old Sonji Roi, a coloured Chicago model who had promised to be converted to the Muslim faith. The wedding took place in Gary in Indiana and no pressmen were permitted to attend. Afterwards the world champion announced that he would retire after the return fight with Liston: "My wife wants me to get out while I'm still pretty". All that Liston did in the long waiting period between their two fights was to earn himself a fine for drunken driving and being in possession of a revolver.

The second Clay *v* Liston fight was to have one further set-back before it could be finalised. Just a fortnight before it was due to take place, the threat of a grand jury investigation caused the promoters to hurriedly seek another site. Antipathy had been boiling up in Boston as the date of the fight drew near and when Garrett Byrne, the city's district attorney, asked for a court restraining order to prevent the contest taking place in Massachussetts on the ground that the promoters were not properly licenced, there was a quick change of venue into the neighbouring State of Maine, the site being the St. Dominic's Youth Centre in Lewiston, a town of 41,000 inhabitants.

Contests for the world's heavyweight

title have been held in strange places, but this one seemed unbelievable and only made possible because of television. A mere 2,434 attended and of these 1,510 were complimentary. Yet the revenue from closed circuit television, radio and other ancillaries brought in 1,602,192 dollars, of which the two contestants shared equally 50 per cent. Why the champion was content to earn as much as his opponent has never been explained.

As usual Ali held the stage from the time of his arrival in Lewiston to the moment he left it. His press conferences were of the usual pattern and his behaviour at the weigh-in only slightly less flamboyant than his antics in Miami, with Liston having to absorb abuse and ridicule, but taking little notice of his opponent's ceaseless ranting. When Ali wagged a finger at him and said: "This time I am going to knock you out", Liston merely wagged a finger back. All along he had been told that he would not last ten rounds. "You tried to blind me in our first fight. You fought dirty and this time you'll find me even dirtier", Ali threatened.

He scaled a trim 206 pounds (14 st. 10 lbs.) with Liston the heavier by 9¼ lbs. When he learned that Sonny was a slight favourite to win at 6 to 5, the champion vigorously protested that this was ridiculous: "I should be at least 7 to 1 to keep my title", he shouted. Unusual rules for the administration of the contest prevailed in Maine. The appointed referee was Jersey Joe Walcott, a former heavyweight champion, but he had no say in deciding who was the winner, acting solely as Third Man, while the points scoring was left in the hands of three judges, Joe Bolvin, Coley Welch and Russell Leonard, all from Maine. As it happened the sole arbitrator of the contest was the knockdown timekeeper, Francis McDonough.

If the first fight had ended in sensational turmoil, it was exceeded as a fiasco by the second, where the action was confined to the official time of exactly one minute. From the starting bell, the champion used the ring, while the challenger attacked, going forward in a shuffling, ponderous manner, jabbing out a long left and endeavouring to get close enough to swing to the body. Meanwhile, Ali was flicking a left to the head and whipping in rights, his blows coming fast, but not seemingly with any great power. Sonny was trying to pin his rival against the ropes, the champion recoiled into them, then bounced back with a hard right to the jaw. A left to the face from Liston was followed by a heavy right to the ribs. Ali flashed a short right to the jaw and to everyone's amazement Liston sank down like a felled ox.

Landing on his back, his arms beyond his head, Sonny did not move and Ali, who had been walking about the ring his gloves held high in token of victory, now stood over his prostrate rival, a terrifying snarl on his lips as he yelled: "Get up, get up you bum". Liston made no move. If he had he would doubtless have been subjected to a merciless blasting against which he would have been helpless. The noise from the excited fans was deafening and Referee Walcott seemed temporarily at a loss to know what action to take. His correct procedure was to order Ali to a neutral corner, then take up the count from the knockdown timekeeper.

51

"Get Up You Bum" the newly-named Muhammad Ali roars at the recumbent Liston, who was declared the loser by a knockout in the 'official' time of 60 seconds in the return title fight at Lewiston.

Instead, he wasted valuable time in arguing with the berserk champion, even trying to use force to get him away from the still reclining Sonny, who had now rolled over into a prone position, his arms extended.

Ali was behaving like a demented person, obviously enjoying the opportunity to put on his favourite act. Eventually he allowed himself to be pushed back, by which time Sonny had risen to his feet, whereupon Walcott wiped his gloves in the customary manner, but suddenly realised that the timekeeper was striving frantically to gain his attention. Sensing something was amiss, Jersey Joe went over to the ropes where he was informed that the fight was over. "I've counted him out twice", said Mr. McDonough. The now thoroughly agitated Third Man turned back to the fighters, there being an even louder outburst from the fans who were delighted to see that Ali and Liston were now swapping punches in a close-range free-for-all mix-up. Back bounded Walcott to bravely go between them, send Sonny to his corner and raise the champion's right arm aloft as the winner. All bedlam broke loose and amidst prolonged booing Liston made his way back dejectedly to the dressing-rooms, while Ali yelled and gesticulated to a mixed storm of cheering and jeering.

The official time of the action was given as sixty seconds precisely, but this was sheer guesswork and quite incorrect, as the televised running of the actual contest took 1 min. 42 secs. A lot of criticism was levelled at the fifty-one-year old Walcott, who was not an experienced referee, for his handling of the bout and it was quite obvious that he had lost his head in the sudden and sensational manner in which the affair ended. But Timekeeper McDonough blamed the champion for the confusion: "If that bum Clay had gone to a neutral corner instead of running around like a maniac all the trouble would have been avoided", he told the press. "I started my stop-watch when I saw Liston hit the canvas and banged off the count until the watch showed that twelve seconds had lapsed when I shut it off. When Jersey Joe came over to me I told him this, also that in my view Liston had stayed down

twenty seconds in all. I made it clear that Sonny had been counted out. Walcott then turned back to the centre of the ring where the fighters had resumed battling, separated them and declared Clay the winner." McDonough, a retired linotype operator, continued: "It was a right to the chin that dropped Liston—a real beauty. There was no doubt in my mind that Sonny had been hurt and hurt badly as he dropped to the canvas. I do not blame Walcott for not taking up the count because he had his hands full trying to cope with Clay. I haven't the slightest doubt that the outcome would have been the same had the fighters been permitted to resume. Liston was so badly hurt that Clay could have killed him".

My own view is that the referee should have warned the champion that he would ignore the count until he obeyed his orders and went to a neutral corner. Referee Dave Barry did that 39 years earlier when Jack Dempsey wanted to stand over the stricken Gene Tunney. The champion would have been in grave danger of being disqualified if a British referee had been ignored in the way Ali treated Walcott. By the time Muhammad had been brought to his senses, Liston would have been on his feet, the Third Man could have decided whether or not he was fit to resume the contest and the fiasco of Lewiston would have been averted.

Controversy over the short-lived heavyweight championship contest raged for some considerable time, Liston being disgraced into temporary retirement, many States declaring that he would never again be granted a licence to box in their territory. The W.B.A. continued to recognise Ernie

Terrell as champion and when it was suggested that Ali's next opponent would be the former champion, Floyd Patterson, the match was outlawed. Ali went about his business irregardless of censure and criticism. He reminded everyone that he was the greatest heavyweight champion of all time. There were rumours that most of the fighter's savings had been handed over to the Muslim movement and it was clear that every effort would be made to enable him to earn as much as possible for the further financial benefit of the champion's religious beliefs. A proposed match with Oscar Bonavena of the Argentine to take place in Tokyo was vetoed, and soon it seemed that the only place left for another title fight would be the Nevada gambling city of Las Vegas.

Meanwhile, although he was kept busy in making public appearances and being featured on radio and television, Ali was having domestic difficulties, finding it increasingly difficult to keep his wife to a strict observance of Muslim beliefs. Shortly after the Liston match she was complaining that they had enjoyed little home life since their marriage and that he could think of nothing but planning more contests. A little later she stated that she had left her husband and was considering divorce. Commenting on this, Ali remarked: "Reconciliation with my wife depends entirely on her. We Muslims don't discuss our private lives, but everything else must step aside for the religion, including a wife and children." On June 22 1965 he filed an application in a Miami court seeking either annulment or divorce, on the grounds that she had refused to keep her promises to adopt his Muslim

beliefs. He complained that her style of dressing failed to live up to the modesty code of his religion. He said that while he was training for a fight Sonji had worn a denim suit with tight pants: "You could see all of her. Tight pants around all those men was wrong." Another time he found her wearing lipstick and scrubbed it off her with a washrag. Asked whether the knee-length, high-neck dress that his wife was wearing in court was acceptable, he burst out: "No, it's too tight. Her knees are showing and her limbs are showing. She's wearing false eyelashes and lipstick." The judge awarded his wife a temporary allowance of 350 dollars weekly, plus the sum, of 2,500 dollars to meet her lawyers' fees. They were divorced on January 11, 1966.

Although he had frequently referred to Floyd Patterson as 'that girl' and called him 'Rabbit', it now suited his purpose to regard the former champion as the only man capable of giving himself a fight. "What Boxing needs is a White Hope, like they were looking for in the days of Jack Johnson. They must find someone they think can lick me, like George Chuvalo, the Canadian champion. Patterson is the white man's black hope. Now that I have disposed of Liston, who was the Rabbit's jinx, he can have a chance to make boxing history by winning the championship for the third time."

That he was being urged to enter into a fight with Patterson was evident when Ali asked the W.B.A. to lift its ban so that he could defend his title in Las Vegas on November 22. He did this on the assurance that such a request would meet with a sympathetic hearing. Eventually the Association gave the proposed Ali *v* Patterson match the all-clear, but made it plain that they would not countenance a 'return fight' clause in the contract; that Ernie Terrell was still regarded as the official world champion, and with the expectancy that Ali would meet Terrell in a match to clear up the undesirable situation that they themselves had created.

The position was clarified when it was announced that Terrell would defend his W.B.A. title against Chuvalo at Toronto on November 1, with the winner being expected to meet the Ali *v* Patterson winner in due course. If the W.B.A. imagined that a Terrell *v* Ali bout would follow automatically, they were due for disappointment as matters turned out. They should have remembered that when asked if he had made any overtures to the W.B.A. to be reinstated as the 'official' world's heavyweight champion, Ali was quoted as saying: "Man, I don't care nothing about them. The internal revenue service and the world recognises and knows I'm the champ."

6. Champion of Champions

If there was any other reason for the urgency in meeting Patterson, it was the desire on Ali's part to put up a performance worthy of a real world-beater. He had procured nothing but scorn from the two enigmatical jousts with Liston, the only glorification having come from his own gushing lips. His public image had been far from popular and this was emphasised when the majority of fight followers wished for a Patterson victory, even though they had small faith in Floyd's ability to beat a man vastly bigger than himself, seven years younger and probably faster.

The critics pointed out that the challenger was much more experienced, having fought 48 times in 13 years against Ali's 21 in five years. In addition, Floyd had boxed 41 rounds in his last five bouts, whereas the champion's ring work had totalled only seven rounds over the same period of time. Since losing his title Patterson had beaten Sante Amonti, Eddie Machen and Tod Henning in Stockholm, George Chuvalo in New York and Charlie Powell in San Juan. At 30 he was in perfect physical shape with boxing still his sole motive in life. Although 52 of the 58 pressmen who sat round the ringside in the ultra-modern Convention Hall at Las Vegas predicted a win for Muhammad, all were of the opinion that Patterson would give a good account of himself and that the fight would not be short-lived. For once the Fighting Prophet did not qualify the round in which the contest would end, although he said more than once, in fact almost continuously, that he would win decisively.

The State of Nevada was not inexperienced in world heavyweight title bouts, Patterson having lost to Liston in Las Vegas two years earlier. In early fight history the State had been a haven for the 1897 contest in which Bob Fitzsimmons defeated Gentleman Jim Corbett in Carson City, while Tex Rickard had been glad to find similar hospitality in Reno, when every other State closed its doors on his Jack Johnson v James J. Jeffries battle in 1910. The Patterson v Ali fight was scheduled for 15 rounds in a 20 ft. ring, the larger size being best suited for the champion's scamperings, giving him 144 extra square feet over the usual 16-footers. The rule whereby three knockdowns in a single round would end the contest was waived, but there would be a mandatory count of 'eight' which would not be started until the other boxer had gone to a neutral corner, thus avoiding a repetition of the Maine fiasco. No return fight clause was allowed in the contract.

The challenger did his final training at the

Thunderbird Hotel, while the champion set up camp in the Stardust Hotel, but first of all insisting that the neon sign over the door advertising him as Cassius Clay should be removed and his new name Muhammad Ali substituted. His so-called workouts were sheer farces as he clowned through them, sharply in contrast to Patterson's intense preparation which appeared pathetic. As evidence of his low opinion of Patterson as an adversary, Ali took time off from his training to fly to Phoenix in Arizona for some spiritual advice from the Muslim leader, Elijah Muhammad.

Referee Harry Krause started them off before a paid attendance of 7,402 fans, but in keeping with the times, millions watched the fight on television. The revenue, after deduction of taxes, amounted to 1,100,000 dollars, of which the champion took 40 per cent and his opponent half that amount. The opening round was quiet, with Patterson coming forward in leaping bursts of action, while Ali used the ring and kept well out of range. Floyd got through with some swift but nonconsequential punches, while the champion did not land a single blow. Ali exerted himself more in the second round,

In the second defence of his world crown Ali demolished a game Floyd Patterson in 12 rounds at Las Vegas. Here he shows no mercy to the ageing ex-champion, who twice won the title.

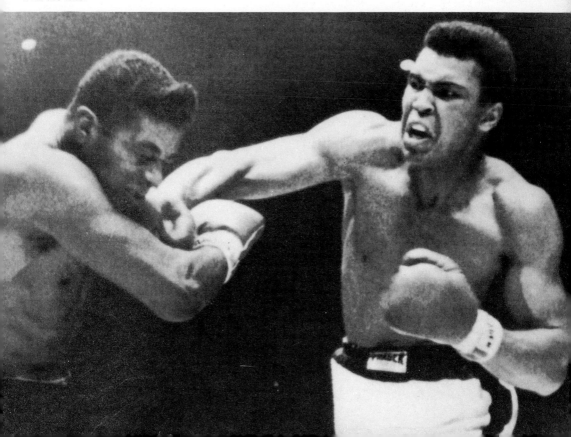

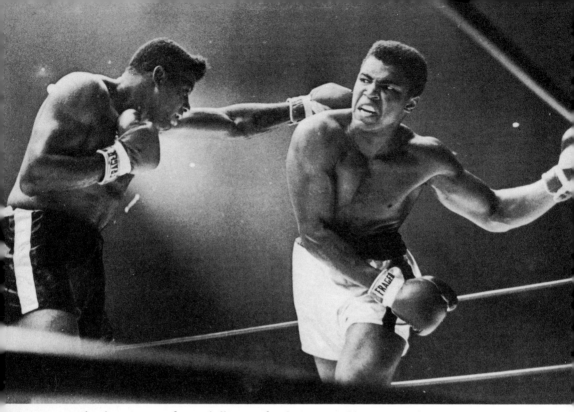

The champion was far too belligerent for the 30-year-old Patterson, showing unusual aggression against a man he had nicknamed 'The Rabbit' and to whom he referred as 'that girl'.

scoring with some lefts that looked light but unsettled the challenger, who tossed a left jab, missed and fell to the canvas. There was no count. Ali took the round with persistent left jabbing and Floyd found it difficult to do more than land on the bigger man's arms and gloves.

The third round showed clearly that it was no match. Muhammad's longer reach enabled him to punish his opponent at will. He landed a series of lefts without retaliation and just before the end put over a sharp right that caught Patterson in the eye. The impact spurred Floyd, who jumped in with a good left hook to the jaw, the one punch to which The Greatest had always been open. The next two rounds provided little excitement beyond making the spectators wonder how much Patterson could take. There seemed little weight behind Ali's blows, but Floyd was wasting a lot of energy in trying to get in a decisive punch. He did land several good lefts to the jaw, but they ran off Muhammad like water.

A stiff left to the chin put the challenger down in round six. He got up to take the mandatory count of 'eight' and went straight into the attack. But his efforts were feeble and got less and less as the rounds went by, with the champion putting in precision punches in almost lackadaisical manner. Patterson's left eye was puffing up and although he was straining nerve and sinew to do something, he could achieve little whilst being steadily cut down to a standstill. From the seventh round onwards Floyd walked back to his corner, one glove pressed into his back and it was obvious that he was in pain. Yet this game fellow stuck out his punishment against a methodical torturer until during the interval following the 11th round, he was visited by the ringside doctor and asked by the referee if he wished to go on. Floyd nodded, but took such a one-sided hammering as Ali set up a savage attack that the bout was halted in 2 min. 18 secs. of the round. While the Third Man conveyed Patterson back to his seconds, so Muhammad announced himself as the winner by walking round the ring, his arms held aloft. He stayed in the ring for 15 minutes after Patterson had left, delivering a long impassioned oration before finally heading for the dressing-room.

There is one aspect of Muhammad's character that makes an epilogue to his fight with Patterson. In a taped interview two months later he stated that he had 'carried' Floyd longer than he originally intended. "The fight should have been stopped at the end of the sixth round", he added. "Are you saying that you 'carried' him for six further rounds?" he was asked. "Well, yes", Ali answered. "I am showing you good boxing. You'd be the first to condemn me for killing him cruelly. He has got beautiful children and I wouldn't want

to hurt him just for the pleasure of the audience. I beat him with my creative and scientific ability and not by punching him too hard."

Anxious to get in as many championship fights as possible in the shortest time, negotiations were entered into for Ali to meet Ernie Terrell, the man who held the W.B.A. version of the world crown. It was a match that both men wanted for obvious reasons, although Muhammad referred to Terrell as the challenger, whereas Ernie regarded himself as on equal terms. Ali's call-up for national service was looming again and he had been in trouble for 'making unpatriotic remarks' to pressmen, after he had been informed that his Army grading had been changed from 1Y to 1A. New York would not consider a match with Terrell on the grounds that the W.B.A. man had underworld associates and although a date was fixed for it to take place in Chicago, it was thrown out when Ali refused to apologise for his anti-Vietnam statement. The venue was then changed to Toronto, but Terrell objected to the terms that were offered and withdrew from the contest. George Chuvalo was brought in as substitute, whereupon the World Boxing Association refused to recognise the contest as involving the world crown as they did not consider the Canadian champion a worthy contender.

There were 13,918 fans in the Maple Leaf Arena and if they did not see a sensational fight they were treated to a dour struggle for the full fifteen rounds, the longest distance Ali had been forced to go in his entire career. It was that combination of fighter versus boxer that always produces a

Tough George Chuvallo, the Canadian champion, twice went the schedule distance with Ali, the first time for the world crown. (*Left*) Muhammad avoids a savage left hook. (*Right*) Counter-punching an attack from his challenger while on the ropes.

hard fight, and if the challenger emerged from it with a swollen and bloodied face and the champion came out without a scratch, it did not imply that Chuvalo had been nothing more than a human punchbag. He had attacked from start to finish, wading in to swing both hands to the body, and although outclassed at long range, was always a potential danger.

There were no knockdowns, but Ali staggered his man on more than a dozen occasions with telling shots to the chin,

while midway through the last round the Canadian surprised his fleet-footed rival with a looping left to the jaw that almost knocked him off his feet. But no doubt the titleholder was feeling the effects of 45 minutes of unceasing pressure by that time. Three times Referee Jackie Silvers cautioned Chuvalo for tossing low blows, but these were not intentional and probably caused by the champion rising to them as he endeavoured to get out of range.

Ali had made no prediction as to the

result, but for once he received unstinted praise for his victory, in that he proved he could stand up to a rugged, determined fighter, who absorbed his best punches and allowed no moments for any relaxed clowning. Muhammad had been kept on his toes for the full duration of each round and had come through the ordeal to win conclusively and in true champion fashion. It was a unanimous verdict with the referee and both judges scoring wide margins in Ali's favour. He had weighed his heaviest yet at 15 st. 4½ lbs., the 28-year old Canadian being 1½ lbs. heavier. The champion's purse, including his share of the ancillary rights, amounted to 340,000 dollars or 50 per cent. He had well earned his money for after the battle he disclosed that both his hands were bruised and swollen: "Chuvalo's head is the hardest thing I have ever punched", he admitted. "I hit him seven or eight good punches, but I had to back off because he's so strong and you can just wear yourself out against a guy like that."

Ali also intimated that negotiations had been afoot some time for a meeting with Henry Cooper in London and in Chicago towards the end of April, he signed to meet the British champion for promoter Harry Levene at Highbury Stadium, home of the Arsenal Football Club, on May 21, just 53 days after the Chuvalo date. He was guaranteed 280,000 dollars, plus U.S. rights to television, radio and movie receipts. Cooper's earnings were said to be in the region of £50,000. It was a match that set England alight, Cooper's host of admirers remembering the time, three years earlier, when 'Our 'Enery' had sent The Greatest sprawling with his famous 'Ammer. 42,400 spectators crowded into the famous football stadium on a pleasant May evening, parting with an estimated £300,000, and hoping against hope that the British champion's tender facial skin would not let him down as it had on the first occasion. They came, eager to see if Cooper could put the champion on the deck for the full count and so bring into British keeping the world heavyweight crown after a gap of 67 years.

The first thing that trainer Dundee did on hearing that the second Cooper v Ali fight was confirmed, was to hang up in the champion's gymnasium in Miami a blown-up photograph of Muhammad on his back, when Henry almost knocked him out. "That's to remind him to cut out the clowning for this fight", said Angelo. Again Ali did not make a prophetic ending to the fight, but he did send Cooper a poem on his 32nd birthday that read: "After I've finished whipping you, you'll think that you are forty-two. Happy Birthday. Your London Bridge will fall down." Ali was given a tremendous reception in London, being a special guest of the Boxing Writers' Club when he was presented with a membership tie. He was strangely quiet and when asked what his defence would be against Henry's left hook, replied: "Stay out of the way of it."

Live presentation of the contest to a number of cinemas was made by Viewsport under the direction of Jarvis Astaire, there was a radio broadcast, while a film version was made for subsequent showing. At the weighing-in ceremony at mid-day thousands tried to get into the Odeon Cinema in Leicester Square. There could not have been more people if royalty were on view. At 13 st. 6 lbs. the British champion was lighter by almost a stone, in fact, he looked somewhat dwarfed against the height and muscularity that made Ali appear to be a god carved in ebony. Referee was George Smith from Edinburgh, who started them off at 10.15p.m. The champion was a hot favourite to win at odds ranging from 5 to 1 to 8 to 1.

The contest followed much the same pattern as their first encounter with Cooper carrying the attack to the champion who was content to keep at long-range, warding off his opponent's punches, then coming in with bursts of rapid punching. All the time he was at distance, Ali jabbed a long left into his rival's face or dabbed over a right, but there was not a lot of power behind his shots, at any rate, Cooper was never badly jarred by them. All the while Henry could avoid cuts he was in the fight with a big chance. He well won the first round, not only on aggression, but because of the punches he got through the champion's defence. But he was never able to land his dynamic left hook and although Muhammad did walk around with his gloves down, it was only when he was well out of striking range. Ali was irritatingly calm and collected while the determined Cooper prodded to the body with his left and tried to work his way in to score with his hooks. But Ali evaded or blocked the blows, scored with light punches, and negatived Henry's work at close range by pushing his head down.

In the second the challenger surprised his rival by repeatedly throwing his right through the champion's guard. Ali had been very watchful of Henry's left, now he

was finding that the Britisher was not a one-hand fighter. Egged on by the big crowd, Cooper attacked with great confidence, but on the few times he got through with a good punch, it had little effect. Ali was guilty of holding whenever danger threatened and was warned for it. There was a good deal of hitting in holds during the third round, for which both were cautioned. Up to now neither of them were showing signs of trouble or having been in a fight for that matter.

Things livened up more in the fourth, both putting more behind their blows with Cooper seemingly desperate to do something dramatic. It was like hitting a shadow, however, except when Ali chose to come back with precision counter-blows, one right to the head towards the close of the round shaking up the Englishman. It must have been very frustrating for Henry, who was putting so much into his work without achieving anything against this india-rubber champion. Henry was most successful with rights to the body, which Ali did not appreciate at all, indeed on one occasion, he looked complaining at the referee and Cooper was so astonished at this gesture on the part of the world champion that he missed a great opportunity to leap in and plant a left hook on Ali's unguarded chin.

The sixth round had been under way only a short while when Ali drew a lead from Cooper then came back with a fast left and following right that connected sharply on the Britisher's left eyebrow. Blood spurted spontaneously from a jagged cut, the gore coming in a stream down Henry's face, converting it into a red mask in a matter of seconds. Referee Smith stopped the contest

When he went to London to defend his championship against Henry Cooper, Ali was presented with a silver trophy by the Boxing Writers' Club.

Cooper's bid for the world heavyweight championship fails at the Arsenal F.C. Stadium, Highbury, in 1966, when again a lacerated eyebrow caused the referee's intervention during the 6th round.

In very serious vein. Ali watches the film of his title fight with Henry Cooper at Highbury in 1966.

and examined the wound, then waved them together for the fight to be continued. Realising that he was in desperate plight, Cooper launched a vicious attack that drove the champion into the ropes. Here Ali fired back some brisk punches at his rival's bloody visage and at once it was obvious that the contest could not be allowed to continue. The Third Man intervened in 1 min. 38 sec. of the round and Muhammad Ali had kept his crown.

Almost immediately it was announced that the next challenger for the world title would be the European champion, Karl Mildenberger, but before that could take

place, the irrepressible Jack Solomons had stepped in with a guarantee of 252,000 dollars for Ali to defend his title against Brian London at the Exhibition Hall at Earl's Court on August 6. Muhammad was due to meet the German on September 10, but the London offer was something that could not be missed, so it was decided to squeeze in both contests.

The less said about the London fight the better, for the former British champion put up a pathetic display that saw him counted out in round three. He had been given as much encouragement as Cooper had received from British followers, the

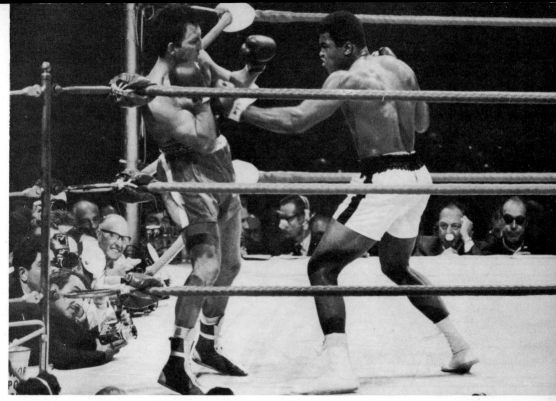

A vicious assault on Brian London in a title defence at Earl's Court, London in 1966.

somewhat disappointing audience of 13,540 that filled only two-thirds of the big arena, giving him unstinted support from the moment he entered the ring. Brian was a notably tough man, a rugged fighter, but with plenty of boxing skill, a man who had bludgeoned his way through many a gruelling brawl. Surely, he would give the champion plenty to think about. He did for the first minute of the fight when, urged on by the chanting crowd, he sailed into Ali as if he had nothing to beat, bustling him into the ropes as if he was going to pummel him out of the ring.

It looked as if there might be an upset, until Muhammad flashed back his first flurry of counter-punches, after which London did not want to know. He beat a steady retreat, his arms wrapped round his head, backed into the ropes and looked spellbound as the increasingly confident Ali punched him at will with both hands before bringing him down early in the third round with some sizzling jaw punches. London did not move while Referee Harry Gibbs counted him out, then the fans, who had changed from cheers to jeers, booed the once-termed Blackpool Blockbuster out of the ring. Millions listened in to this fiasco, it was beamed to America in colour for the

E

first time in boxing history. Yet it was something everyone was glad to forget.

Promoter Levene and Joachim Gottert, with the aid of Viewsport, staged the Ali *v* Mildenberger title fight at the Wald Festhall Stadium in Frankfurt 35 days after the Earl's Court disaster. They paid Ali a guarantee of 250,000 dollars, plus 50 per cent of all ancillary rights and were rewarded with an attendance of 29,600 who paid 652,000 dollars between them. Many G.I.s stationed in the city were among the spectators. At 28 the German had won 49 of his 54 fights with two losses. Dark-haired and good-looking he was square-set, heavily muscled, durable and a hard puncher, having won the E.B.U. title by knocking out Sante Amonti, of Italy, in a single round.

He was the first southpaw (right-foot foremost boxer), ever to fight for the world crown and as it was generally known that Ali was uneasy against men who led with the right, it was thought that the West German would not be an easy man to beat. Muhammad was very subdued both in pre-fight interviews and at the weigh-in, a ceremony he usually reserved for a hearty spell of play-acting. Referee was Teddy Waltham, general secretary to the British Boxing Board of Control, himself a former boxer.

After a feeling-out opening round, Karl stepped up the pace and Ali responded. It was fast work for heavies, with the German puzzling his opponent by getting through with right jabs to the body. He also hooked well with a strong left and the world champion made good use of the ring in his customary manner, shooting out punches from either hand and putting in the occasional burst of combination blows. He was using his right more than usual (the perfect answer to a southpaw) especially as an uppercut which he swept through the shorter man's glove cover. The challenger was giving the American a tough fight and whereas he seemed on the verge of putting his rival down, Ali did not appear to have hurt Mildenberger, although the German was bleeding from a small cut under the left eye at the end of round four.

The pace had slowed a little as they came out for the fifth. The German continued to attack, but now Ali was catching him with superb right crosses as he advanced, one fine punch worsening the wound under Mildenberger's eye, while another toppled him over for a count of 'one' just before the bell sounded. The sight of blood appeared to enrage the champion as he set about his challenger with great gusto, hitting him almost at will and bringing blood from his nose to further redden his face. Mildenberger was still fighting resolutely, but Ali had his measure now and only grim courage and superb fitness kept the German on his feet. In the eighth, Muhammad dropped his man with a telling right that caused Karl to turn a complete somersault and although he was up at 'six' a mandatory count was taken. Then Karl was driven into a corner and belaboured freely, the bell seemingly saving him from being knocked out.

Ali boxed with coolness and assurance, punishing the West German with regularity, disregarding any blows that Mildenberger managed to get through to the body. It was fast becoming 'no contest' and when Ali caught his durable challenger with a magni-

(Left) The former British champion (Brian London) taking the full count in round three.

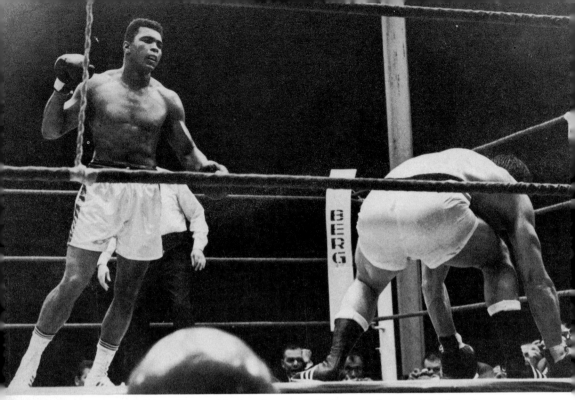

In the sixth defence of his world title, Ali stopped the European heavyweight champion, Karl Mildenberger, of West Germany, seen taking a count, in the 12th round of their Frankfurt contest.

ficent right in round ten, the end did not seem far off. Karl took six seconds to rise, was kept standing for another two and the now one-sided match went on. In the 11th, Referee Waltham stopped the contest and told the champion to close his gloves. "Which one?" asked Ali and he was told "Both". "Okay, sir", he responded and immediately caught Mildenberger with some hard punches and soon the German was bleeding from a cut between his nose and right eye. He came out gamely for the 12th but looked tired and dejected. Ali had had enough. He staggered his challenger with a solid right to the chin, then swept in

a mighty left uppercut that had his man groggy. The German was helpless and Referee Waltham immediately stepped between them. The bout was ended in 1 min. 30 secs. of the round and Muhammad Ali was the winner and still champion. He had come out of the encounter without a mark to show he had been in a fast, hard fight.

Back in America, Ali lost no time in announcing that he would be defending his title against Cleveland Williams, of Houston in Texas, in two months time, would have a rest and then take on Ernie Terrell—to prove who was the real world champion.

The choice of Houston had a three-fold purpose. In the first place it was Williams' home-town, while Muhammad had also moved there from Louisville. The remaining factor was that the city now possessed a vast Astrodome, really a roofed-in open-air arena capable of containing 66,000. It was claimed to be the Eighth Wonder of the World. Here Ali was guaranteed another 235,645 dollars (approximately £100,000) with once more 50 per cent of the revenues additional to the live gate money.

For once the champion would be boxing a man taller than himself (by one inch) and with a slightly longer reach. At 15 st. 2¾ lbs., the champion had a small advantage of 2¼ lbs. over his challenger, but of more importance was the disparity in their ages, Ali at 24, being the younger by nine years. Williams, whom they called 'The Big Cat', had a pro record extending over 15 years. It contained many inside-the-distance wins, including one over Terrell, but twice he had lost to Sonny Liston in quick time. In spite of everything, it was no match. Ali did as he pleased, dropped Williams three times in the second round, the last time leaving him stretched out on the canvas like a giant star-fish, the bell coming to his rescue. He should not have been sent up for the third which was all over in 68 seconds, Referee Harry Kessler calling a halt after the challenger had been floored with a magnificent right cross and, having beaten the count, was stumbling round the ring under a hail of hooks.

The largest crowd ever for an indoor fight 35,460, paid 461,290 dollars but there were 37,321 in attendance three months later when Ali met Terrell in a contest that was universally recognised as for the world crown. There was no doubt in the minds of most boxing followers that Muhammad Ali was the rightful owner of the world heavyweight title, solely because he had beaten the reigning champion, whereas Terrell had been merely nominated to that exalted position by the World Boxing Association, which did not control the sport throughout the entire fistic world.

Ali could have ignored Terrell, but pride would not allow him to countenance a usurper to his throne. Moreover, the W.B.A. champion had blamed Ali for the deadlock that had prevented them from

'Big Cat' Cleveland Williams lasted only three rounds in his title chance against Ali at Houston, being saved by the referee.

6 ft. 6 in. Ernie Terrell, whom the W.B.A. recognised as world champion, took an unmerciful physical and mental beating when he met Ali at Houston in 1967. These pictures show dramatically Muhammad avoiding a left hook and countering with a magnificent right to the jaw. He won a unanimous points award.

meeting a lot earlier and he made the grave error of stating publicly that he intended to knock out Muhammad, so that he could devote his entire time to being a Muslim minister. "Let him confine himself to preaching, he's been doing that for years", commented Ernie. The army authorities, however, were not impressed by the new claim of the world champion that as a Muslim minister he was exempt from military service. They said there was no proof that he was a practising minister, whereupon Ali produced 43 statements and 92 petitions signed by 3,810 Muslims that he was a full-time preacher. It seemed that he was determined to avoid soldiering at all cost.

Perhaps the ballyhoo tantrums for this

fight were greater than ever before for a heavyweight battle, but this time Terrell was not a silent partner. There was nearly a fight between them when they were introduced from the ring prior to a fight in Houston, in fact, Ali had to be restrained from striking Ernie, who at 6 ft. 6 ins. towered over The Greatest. He infuriated the champion by persistently calling him 'Cassius Clay' and Ali shouted back that he would make him acknowledge his true name when once they met in combat. "You will eat those words, letter by letter", threatened the Muslim minister. Apart from his extra inches, Terrell had a reach advantage of four inches and relied on his phenomenal 82-ins. to score his victories, his left jab being a soul-destroying weapon that had won him 39 wins in 43 bouts, with 18 stoppages to his credit.

It was reckoned to be a battle of left leads, but actually it was no match at all, for whereas Terrell had to rely on a solitary weapon, Ali had a wide repertoire of punches and moves which he could conduct efficiently at long range. Terrell suffered a humiliating and punishing defeat that the champion allowed to go the full distance, for it seemed that after the eighth round he could have put on an assault that would have battered the big man to the canvas. All through the contest Ali kept shouting at his victim: "What is my name?", "Who am I?", "Who is the Champion of the World?" The more he hurt Terrell, the louder the taunts and it is safe to say that no man has ever been given a more drawn-out methodical battering than that practiced on the W.B.A. Champion. It was not remarkable that Ernie should be on his feet at the finish—he was there because Ali intended his suffering should be ended only by the final bell. It was a sadistic streak that had shown itself only once before, when Muhammad stood over the prostrate Liston in their second fight.

The ninth defence of his world title in three years took place 44 days later when Zora Folley, a built-up contender, faced Ali in Madison Square Garden, New York, before 13,780 fans, who contributed 20,000 dollars less than the champion's guaranteed purse of 264,835.85 dollars. It was estimated at this point that Ali's guaranteed purses from the time of winning the championship amounted to over 3,302,000 dollars, in addition there were the huge sums received from television, radio and film rights, usually 50 per cent of all such earnings. Yet one New York columnist asserted that Muhammad was 'broke', even that he was 'in debt to the Muslim movement'. At the same time Ali was telling everyone that he planned to buy property in Chicago, buy a 50,000 dollar home in Houston and buy a hundred-acre farm in Florida. "I've bin saving of late", he said. "Apart from training expenses, I spent only eight dollars in preparation for my last fight. Come to think of it, I don't know what I spent it on, Must have given it away."

Folley, an experienced boxer of considerable talent, might have stood a chance of beating Ali had the fight taken place five years earlier. Now, at 34, he was conceding nine years and the same number of pounds in weight. For three rounds he made a good showing whilst the champion did little but spar at long range. But in the fourth the champion opened out and a flashing left and right to the chin dropped the challenger flat on his face. He got up at 'four', took a standing count, and was punched freely for the remainder of the round, going to his corner with his nose bleeding. Try as he might Folley could not avoid Ali's straight left jabs and by the seventh round he had been so completely taken apart that when he was floored from an accurate right to the chin, he again struck the floor face downwards and this time was counted out, the round having lasted 1 min. 48 secs. None of those who saw this win as conclusive evidence that Ali was indeed 'The Greatest' were to know that the ring had seen the last of him for over 3½ years.

7. In and Out of the Wilderness

In an effort to reap one more championship harvest to help offset his mounting legal expenses and the alimony payments to his first wife, Ali made haste to sign for a second defence of his title against Floyd Patterson at Las Vegas, a venue highly suitable for a repeat performance because of its constantly changing gambling population. Here, Promoter Harold Conrad, on behalf of a sporting syndicate, was prepared to guarantee the champion 150,000 dollars. The title fight was set to take place on April 25, 1967, just three days prior to the date he was due for induction into the U.S. Army—and the timing was perfect. Unfortunately for Muhammad and his Muslim supporters, however, Governor Paul Laxalt vetoed the bout on the grounds that "it would give Nevada a black eye" and the plan had to be abandoned.

On May 8 he was indicted for violation of the Selective Service Act by a Federal Grand Jury. He pleaded 'not guilty' and was released on bail of five-thousand dollars. He had moved his place of residence from Louisville to Houston in order to delay matters, but on June 20 he appeared in the Texan port before an all-white jury to answer charges of evading national service. His plea that he was an ordained Muslim minister was dismissed. He was convicted of refusing induction into the U.S. Army and given the maximum sentence possible by District Judge Joe Ingraham—imprisonment for five years and a fine of ten-thousand dollars. He remained free, pending an appeal, on the 5,000 dollar bond already paid into court.

Ali stood rigid as the judge handed down the sentence. He showed no emotion when the verdict was read and left the court quickly. But outside he burst forth and told reporters: "I'm the champ. I can beat any man alive. I don't have to prove it to anybody. It doesn't make any difference if they take my name off a few bits of paper. You can't brainwash the fact that I am the champ out of the minds of the people. If I thought it would bring freedom, justice and equality for twenty-two million so-called negroes, they wouldn't have to draft me. I'd join tomorrow."

It now seemed that his days as a professional boxer were ended. He was banned from accepting fights outside the United States, his passport being forfeited. The World Boxing Association refused to recognise him as heavyweight champion of the world, again declaring the title vacant, and one by one the other governing bodies of Boxing followed suit. No matter how hard his lawyers fought to save him from military service, they could not secure him the right to continue the only vocation he knew.

To most men this might have been a desperate situation, but Ali seemed unperturbed. In August 1967 he became married again, his bride being Belinda Boyd, a 17-year old student at the Muslim college in Chicago. Muhammad had a house in the city and the wedding took place there with a selected few in attendance. The service was performed with both Muslim and Christian rites, the best man being Herbert Muhammad, who described himself as Ali's manager, presumably having taken over when the contract with the Louisville syndicate expired. The bride wore a floor length white silk dress while the bridegroom was clad in a black silk suit. He announced that he was going to begin a new life, that henceforth he would occupy himself with preaching his Muslim beliefs.

There is no doubt that at this time in his life Ali must have been in two minds about his future. Whether he would ever be allowed again to box professionally, or if he would have to be satisfied with being a religious preacher, a not unpleasant thought as here was a vocation that invited full flow for his gift of eloquence and also provided a continuous run of public appearances. Impulsive talking and the attention of an audience were his life blood and now he set out to be as good an orator as he had been a boxer, studying and listening for hours to the recorded preachments of Elijah Muhammad, the wizened little leader of the so-called Black Muslims. After a year spent in touring the States in a bus and lecturing to pre-arranged coloured gatherings, he was interviewed in his Chicago home: "It is a beautiful life", he beamed. "I could not give it up, even if it meant going to prison. I've always liked the truth and still do, that is why I have given up the prospect of earning ten-million dollars for what I believe in. Nothing is more satisfying than travelling the country and preaching the word of Allah."

He spoke with some bitterness about his financial state, although his home surroundings did not suggest poverty. "They are trying to break me by not allowing me to fight. I have to pay that woman (his first wife) 1,200 dollars (£500) a month and Haydon Covington, my attorney, who got me the maximum sentence, is suing me for more than 200,000 dollars in costs. How can I have any money?" Does that mean to say you are broke?" he was asked. "Well, I'm not earning any and it costs money to live, so I must be."

Questioned as to his reaction to the efforts being made by the World Boxing Association and the New York State Boxing Commission to establish a new world heavyweight champion, he said: "They can have all the tournaments they want, but they can't have my title until someone beats me for it. A man remains champion until he is whipped, quits or dies. That's the law in Boxing." He added: "I am glad they are finding new championship material. I had beaten them all and when I'm allowed to fight again, I'll take them one by one and beat them." Which suggests that he had not given up all hope that by the subtle use of delaying tactics, the war in Vietnam might have ended or a change made in the national service draft procedure that would ease the

73

pressure and permit his return to the ring.

Washington turned down his appeal out-of-hand, U.S. Attorney Morton Sussman arguing that until Ali found himself confronted with being drafted, he had consistently stated his occupation as 'professional boxer', his claim for deferment on religious scruples was therefore unfounded. This decision was later confirmed by the 5th Circuit of Appeals, which announced: "Being entirely satisfied that Cassius Clay (also known as Muhammad Ali) has been fairly accorded due process of law, and without discrimination, we affirm his conviction." A month later Ali asked for a re-hearing and the affair dragged on until public feeling against him became less and less and the sports writers turned their attention to the eight-man competition being organised by the W.B.A. and the efforts of the rival authority in New York to get in first with a worthy new world champion.

Ali came into the news periodically. In June 1968 a baby daughter was born to him at South Chicago Community Hospital. "She will be a righteous Muslim and live a good, clean life, that's all we pray for", he announced, hiding his disappointment, for he had wished for a son who he could teach and train to be a boxer. In March the following year, he was reported to have spent a ten-day sentence in Dade County jail in Miami for a two-year old traffic violation, being released with fifty other prisoners a few days before Christmas as a goodwill gesture. He had served his time, cut down by three days, in kitchen duties and had apparently enjoyed the experience.

Unexpectedly he came back into the box-

ing scene when someone engaged his services with those of former champion, Rocky Marciano, in a coloured computerized film, made by the aid of still photographs blended together in a process known as 'photomation'. They were made to appear as if fighting for the world title and although both were on the pudgy size, the production was very convincing, even if the sound effects—the swapping of punches—was somewhat over-realistic. Ali was reported to have been paid 9,999 dollars for his part in the production, or ten per cent of the revenue, whichever was greatest, and agreed not to sue if he proved to be the loser. This indemnity was introduced because in a previous computerised version of a fight between himself and former champion James J. Jeffries, he had been returned as beaten, which he claimed as damaging to his reputation. He had sued for a million dollars, but settled for one dollar, his honour having been satisfied.

As the computerised film was shown all over the world, Ali's image was resurrected and the fight fraternity began to wonder what might happen if he was given the chance to meet Joe Frazier, now recognised as world champion in New York. Ali squashed such speculation when he told students at Wayne State University; "I'm completely finished with boxing and all sports." Hardly were the words out of his mouth when things began to happen to the contrary. His lawyer's claim was dismissed and in October 1969 Ali was granted a licence to box by the Mississippi State Athletic Commission.

On receiving intimation of this favourable move, he immediately seized the opportunity to assume his leadership of the heavyweight championship. "Frazier has said he would fight me if I got a licence. Well, bring on Frazier, because I have now got one." Such a contest would necessitate Ali receiving a licence to box in New York State and he moved into the picture for such an event by accepting the title role in a play entitled *Big Time Buck White* at the George Abbott Theatre on Broadway. It was a musical about a Black Power leader, and did not enjoy great success. But it put Ali back into the public mind.

In spite of these favourable moves, Muhammad could not have been too sure about an eventual return to the ring, on the other hand he might have been purposely showing a disinclination to resume boxing merely to arouse more interest. At the Stanley Theatre in Philadelphia for the initial showing of the computerised fight with Marciano, the result of which had been kept secret, Ali shouted: "If I lose this it proves that the film was made in Alabama", and afterwards, the film ending with Ali being knocked out in the 13th round, he stated: "It's time I quit when a 45-year old man beats me," and when asked about his future, he replied: "I will never fight again." For the record, Marciano never knew the result of the computerised contest as he had been killed in an air crash a short while previous to the film's premier.

There was one further denial which came following the contest between Frazier and Jimmy Ellis, Ali's former sparring-partner, who had won the W.B.A. tournament and also claimed the championship. The pair met at Madison Square Garden in New York and the fight ended in round four,

Referee Tony Perez calling a halt when Ellis was on the canvas having been battered into helplessness. Immediately afterwards Ali announced that he had handed over the title to Frazier: "I will never fight again", he vowed. "Boxing needs me, but I no longer need boxing. My hands are clean, I owe no taxes to Uncle Sam. I am not putting all my eggs into one basket in future. The bread will come from the book I'm writing—my life story; the butter from the stage; and the cream from films. After the computer fight a company realised my acting potential because, after all those fights I've had, there are no scratches or scars on my face."

His financial future seemed secure. He had made a 'racial' disc called "All over now, mighty Whitey." and was also earning from commercial television advertising, appearing on discussion programmes, and from lecturing to college students. That he had been paid a sixty-thousand dollar grant on an autobiography of which not a word had been written, was perhaps the highest proof of the amazing pulling power of this unique personality. Yet it is probable that in his own country the majority of people disliked him.

By September 1970 Ali had been sentenced for draft evasion for over three years, yet had not gone to prison or paid the imposed fine. Nor had he fought in that time or done any serious training, beyond his inborn urge to keep himself in good physical shape. This negative state of affairs might have gone on indefinitely had not the Supreme Court, which had upheld his conviction, suddenly declared a reverse ruling to the effect that young men who opposed war on strong ethical grounds should be exempted from drafting into the armed forces. It was a surprise decision that delighted the fight fraternity. Those behind Muhammad, together with the businessmen of boxing, immediately laid plans for his forthright return to the ring. It is conceivable that the exiled champion had had an inkling of what might be pending and had been preparing himself for such a contingency as, a few months earlier, when Joe Bugner, the promising British heavy, had been in America to gain experience, he had sparred a few rounds with Ali, as he did with Joe Frazier, Sonny Liston and Jimmy Ellis.

There were more talks of a match with Frazier and the way was made clear when Ali was invited to go to New York and undergo a medical examination, the passing of which would ensure the issuing of a licence to box by the State Athletic Commission. He was found to be fit, both mentally and physically, for a resumption of his boxing career, for even though his weight had risen to 16 st. 2½ lbs. because of enforced idleness, this was only a stone in excess of his best fighting poundage.

Within a few weeks Ali was boxing an eight-round exhibition with three sparring partners at Moorhouse College in Atlanta, Georgia, where Martin Luther King Jr. had been educated. With him, brought specially from Miami to be in his corner, was Angelo Dundee, who said afterwards: "I came here expecting nothing, instead I saw it all. For any other heavyweight it would have taken six months to return from a three-years lay-off. This man is a truly remarkable athlete." Ali had moved with much of his former speed and grace, hands hanging at his sides as he floated round the ring, making his rivals miss and tossing occasional jabs and combinations. The onlookers were greatly impressed and no time was lost in finding an opponent whom the public would accept as capable of testing Ali to the full.

Choice fell on white Jerry Quarry, a Los Angeles heavy who had fought out the final of the W.B.A. tournament with Jimmy Ellis to whom he had lost narrowly on points. Since then he had been stopped by Frazier in seven rounds and by tough George Chuvalo, the Canadian champion, also in seven rounds. But he had won his last four bouts and in a five-year record had been beaten only four times in 45 contests, 23 of which had ended inside the distance, which gave evidence of his punching power. Quarry was both strong and resolute, anxious to fight his way back among the leading heavies. It was thought he might prove too tough a handful for the ring-rusty Muhammad.

The 15-round fight was scheduled to take place in the Municipal Auditorium at Atlanta with Ali securing a guarantee of 750,000 dollars and Quarry 400,000 dollars, just evidence that the former champion still possessed extraordinary drawing power. Although State Governor Lester Maddox tried his hardest to have the bout banned, after talking to Vietnam war veterans, he was over-ruled by State Attorney General Arthur Bolton, who said there was no legal way of stopping the contest from taking place.

In a sparring session with Al 'Blue' Lewis in the winding-up stages of his training, Ali

76

At Atlanta, just before his 1970 comeback contest with Jerry Quarry. Ali pinches his mother's cheek to assure her there is nothing to worry about.

was dumped on the canvas to everyone's amusement. But he was not play-acting as he explained afterwards. "Yes, he knocked the wind out of me", he admitted. "I did not have my muscles properly tensed because I am out of practice. Blue Lewis is about 6 ft. 4 in. and weighs 225 lbs. and a punch from him would hurt anybody." Asked if he would like to predict the out-come of his fight with Quarry, he replied: "I have finished predicting and fooling around. That stuff was merely to sell myself on the way up. I don't need it now. I'm dead serious about this comeback and every-one in the world is waiting to see if I am still The Greatest. After this fight they'll see I am still The Champ."

77

8. The Moment of Truth

With all the physical advantages, $2\frac{1}{2}$ inches in height and over a stone in weight, Ali was made favourite to beat Quarry at the solid odds of 4 to 1. His fine muscular body, brought to perfect condition, made him look a giant against the 25-year old Irish-American, who seemed determined to re-establish himself as a leading contender by stopping the so-far unbeaten ex-champion. He attacked strongly from the start, but found it extremely difficult to get within striking range as his rival kept at distance and used the ring whilst peppering him with left jabs from a six-inch longer reach. Short in the arm, Jerry had to force his way through a withering fire of jabs that soon had his face reddening. Occasionally he got in a stray body punch, but Ali was always moving away and took such blows at half power.

Ali's long range strategy worked beautifully. Quarry lunged and thumped hopefully, but was completely outboxed. A puncher always has a chance and the white fighter was obviously pinning his hopes on keeping the pressure going until the other man tired and he could pin him against the ropes under a barrage of blazing hooks. But Muhammad was too smart and burned up little energy as he glided about the ring and jabbed and jabbed and jabbed.

In the third round it seemed for the first time that Quarry might win. He succeeded in bundling his rival against the ropes for a brief spell and landed a couple of clumps to the body. But Ali leaned back over the top strand and fired two sizzling shots at the head and Jerry came away with blood streaming from a cut over his left eye. Realising that he had been wounded, Quarry fought desperately to bring down the coloured man, but Ali banged in a vicious right-hander that ripped open the cut, causing the gore to cascade down Jerry's face, on to his chest and trunks.

The bell clanged before the referee could intervene or any more damage be caused. But as soon as Quarry's chief second, Teddy Bentham, saw the state of the eye injury, he signalled to Tony Perez that he was stopping the contest. Jerry sprang to his feet and protested vigorously, but the official would not permit him to continue and he went over to Ali's corner and raised his hand as the winner. It took eleven stitches to sew up Quarry's wound.

So the first step in the great comeback had been negotiated successfully although not without some cogitation as to what the result might have been had Quarry not been cut. The former champion had yet to convince the boxing public that he still had the staying power to last out the full championship distance of fifteen-rounds, which would be required if and when he got into the same ring as Joe Frazier, a match for which negotiations were going ahead even while Ali was preparing for his next trial, a match with Oscar Bonavena, a burly Argentine fighter of no great skill, but immense strength and staying power. It seemed that Ali was to be tried very highly for his second comeback appearance, and it was to his credit that he had not tried to win his way back by meeting an array of push-overs.

Certainly Bonavena was not in that category. He had been boxing professionally for seven years and had never been stopped in 53 fights. Of these he had won 46 (37 stopped or knocked out). Twice he had fought Frazier, in their first meeting having Joe down for two counts and losing on a disputed verdict at the end of ten-rounds. Their second meeting had been over fifteen-rounds for Frazier's New York version of the heavyweight title. Again the Argentine fighter had put up a good performance, although being convincingly outpointed this time.

At the New York weigh-in there was a flare-up between Muhammad and Bonavena that was touched off when Oscar accused Ali of being 'chicken' for refusing to go into the U.S. Army. This made the former champion predict that he would dispose of his rival in nine rounds, and whilst many people thought that Ali would win, few, if any, felt that he could punch hard enough to stop the die-hard South American.

The fight proved a near sell-out for Madison Square Garden, with 19,417 fans paying 615,401 dollars, of which Ali was guaranteed 200,000 dollars, plus a share of the ancillary rights from radio, television, etc. At 15 st. 2 lbs. he was at an advantage of six pounds. But he was taller by several inches and had a correspondingly longer reach. The fight was on similar lines to the Quarry encounter, with Ali moving around, refusing to be drawn into punch-swapping and conducting the exchanges from long range.

Bonavena set up a swarming attack which he maintained in every round, tossing his big punches, mainly at the body, and getting through occasionally, but always at a retreating target. Twice he was warned for low blows, one of which appeared to hurt the former champion, but from a boxing point of view it was really no contest, Ali taking every round with something to spare.

When the ninth was due to start the fans began chanting to remind Ali of his pre-diction. He wanted no prompting, in fact, was so anxious to finish the fight that he fell to the canvas after missing with what was intended to be the payoff punch. Up immediately, he drilled into the Argentine boxer with precision blows that came from all angles. Bonavena was shaken time and again by telling rights and set back on his heels from stinging left jabs. His right eye started to close and his nose bled, but he took everything that Ali could hand out in a furious effort to bring him down. Not only did Oscar stay on his feet, he also had the satisfaction of catching Ali with a mighty left hook that sent him staggering. When he got back to his corner Muhammad shook his head and said to his seconds: "He should have gone down." He was bleeding slightly from the mouth and a lot of his confidence seemed to have ebbed away when the bell sounded to start the tenth.

Going back to sheer boxing, Ali resumed control of the contest, peppering the South American with left jabs and right crosses, while Bonavena kept coming forward and lunging away at the body, causing his rival to be continually dancing out of danger. In the 12th Ali seemed to be tiring under the pressure and was constantly guilty of hanging on when Oscar forced his way into a clinch. But the scoring was on Muhammad's side, although it was obvious that he was being extended to the full. He sat in his corner at the end of the 13th round, head bowed, as his handlers massaged his arms and legs. Both were well spent and the next session saw far too much holding and wrestling, the fans getting restless and calling on the two warriors for more action.

They got it in full in the 15th and last round, for Ali came out like a tornado and regardless of defence, had Bonavena bewildered under a fast bombardment of accurate punches that came like machine-gun bullets. Muhammad had been given the fight of his life for fourteen rounds, now he was boxing with speed and fury, as if the bout had just begun and there was nothing to beat. The fans started to roar as they sensed a startling climax, rising to their feet as Ali whipped over a stunning right to the jaw that dropped the durable Bonavena in a heap.

He staggered to his feet at 'eight', but was chopped down again from a burst of two-handed clips to the chin. The towel fluttered

in from the South American's corner, but Referee Mark Conn ignored this signal of surrender and allowed the fight to continue after Oscar had taken a mandatory count. He shaped up to his eager assailant, but Ali did not intend to let him off the hook. A blast of combination punching battered down the gallant South American for the third time. Then, in accordance to New York rules which called for the ending of a contest after three knockdowns in a single round, the Third Man stepped between them and acclaimed Ali as the winner with 57 seconds of the contest still to go.

It was a spectacular victory, well in keeping with Ali's character, and now there was no question in anyone's mind that he had qualified to fight Frazier for the world crown. As was to be expected, Ali regarded Joe as merely another challenger. "He is fighting me, I'm not fighting him for the championship", he repeated in every interview, and there were many who agreed with this sentiment. After all, he had never been beaten for the championship and Frazier had never been regarded as a contender all the while Ali had been the recognised titleholder.

Their coming fight was now inevitable. It was what is known in the Fight Game as a 'natural' and fans all over the world licked their lips at the prospect. It did not matter where it would be fought—in the middle of the Sahara, if necessary—it just had to be staged. It would be televised to every country where Boxing was popular and it was estimated that the total take would exceed ten-million dollars.

Interviewed on an Albuquerque T.V. station, where he and his wife stopped off en route to Los Angeles to visit friends, Ali said that win, lose or draw, it would be his last fight. "I've been in this boxing business for sixteen years and I'm tired. I will clear a million dollars from the Frazier fight and I'm going to invest the money and buy some land, probably in New Mexico. I am the greatest fighter in the world—a real professional. Compared with me, Frazier is a tramp and an amateur."

A bidding war between promoters throughout America ended with the bout secured for Madison Square Garden, both Frazier and Ali being guaranteed 2½-million dollars (over one million pounds). It was possible for this vast amount to be exceeded when the extras were added to the live gate money of 1,352,951 paid by the maximum crowd of 20,455, in fact, the total gross take was estimated at twenty-million dollars. There was the usual verbal punch-up when the pair met for the signing of contracts, with Ali doing most of the shouting, although Joe kept pace with him, promising that the contest would not go the full fifteen-rounds. "If he whips me, I'll get right down on my knees and crawl across the ring and tell him he's the champion", stated Muhammad with finality. "But there is no chance of that", he added. "It will be like a good amateur fighting a class professional, like a kid out of the Olympics facing the fastest heavyweight champion that ever lived. It will be No Contest."

In January 1971 the U.S. Supreme Court cleared the way for the Frazier v Ali fight by agreeing to hear his appeal against his 1967 conviction for draft evasion. The decision, received with relief in boxing circles, lifted the only remaining cloud on the heavyweight horizon and now the papers were freely talking about the coming 'Fight of the Century'. Every seat in Madison Square Garden was sold a month beforehand, as was the accommodation in the numerous cinemas and theatres which planned to screen the contest 'live'. In the United Kingdom over thirty cinemas were booked for viewing, the doors opening at 1 a.m. with the showing at 4.30 a.m. the intervening time being devoted to pre-fight films and interviews.

As usual Ali provided all the publicity, if any was needed, for the success of the occasion. In training at Miami Beach he struck a new line by promising to predict the result of the contest from his dressing-room five minutes before the start by opening a sealed envelope. He also astonished everyone by saying: "I want a fresh referee every round because there ain't no man who can keep up the pace I'm going to set, except me." In almost the same breath he told his listeners; "This fight is going the full distance. I'm training for 15 rounds because I'm going to punish Frazier in every one of them. He ain't got no respect. I told him the day we signed contracts, I would punish him for calling me Clay instead of Ali. I'm going to punish him, too, for calling himself the champion."

An estimated 300 million viewers on television saw Ali open his envelope as promised and announce with all solemnity that Frazier would fall in six. It was a contradiction of his previous prophesy and one he was not to be permitted to make come true. And, as it happens, he came perilously close to not completing the fifteenth and final round himself. But he did

F

provide the one big thrill in a fight that was not as exciting as had been anticipated. At 15 st. 5 lbs., Ali was 9½ lbs. heavier, while he topped Frazier by 3½-inches. These assets, plus the corresponding advantage in reach did not compensate for the years he had spent out of the ring.

Facing a man aptly named the Black Marciano, who had been heavyweight gold medallist in the Tokyo Games, was unbeaten in 26 paid bouts, had defended successfully on five occasions his New York version of the heavyweight title and had stopped Jimmy Ellis in four rounds to become universally recognised as world champion, Ali was given a terrific task. Yet in my view, had he not fooled away some of the middle rounds of the contest, he could have been returned a points winner, despite a paralysing knockdown in the last round.

His plans were well laid, to use the ring and let rugged Frazier chase him from first gong to last. He did this successfully at the start, moving away from a man who had the power and the determination to mow him down with a non-stop deluge of heavy hooks and swings, mainly aimed at the body. So far as Smokin' Joe was concerned, he set out with the sole intention of attacking unceasingly until his opponent wilted under the pressure. He stuck to these tactics, whereas Ali did not rigidly adhere to his.

A ferocious onslaught by Frazier forces Ali to bring out all his defensive resources in order to avoid being knocked out. Here he is in trouble in a corner.

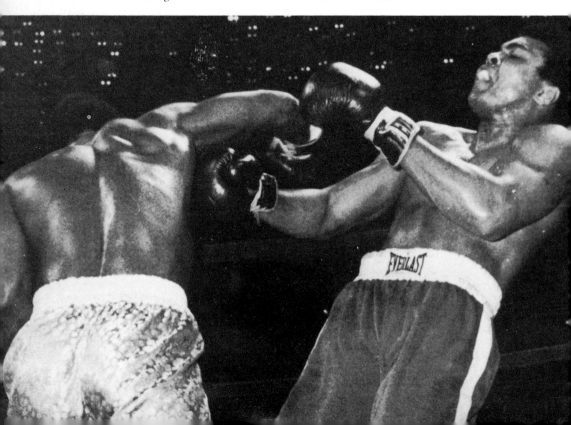

Ali's comeback attempt temporarily halted by a sizzling left hook from Joe Frazier in their exciting New York battle which the champion won on points.

After a flare-up in the fifth round, when obviously the former champion was endeavouring to soften up his opponent for a prophetic victory in the next round, Ali seemed set on lasting the distance rather than trying to win decisively. This he did successfully up to the first minute of the last round when, either because of a momentary lapse in concentration or because he was too weary to concentrate any more, he let Frazier land his favourite left hook to the chin, a mighty punch that sent him sprawling on his back.

It was the Henry Cooper moment all over again, but this time there was no bell to come to the rescue. Instead, Ali got up at 'three', took five more seconds to make up the mandatory count and then had to use every trick and artifice he knew to remain on his feet until the end of the contest.

At the finish he seemed surprised that he had lost, maintaining that he had landed three punches to each one scored by Frazier; that apart from a swollen right jaw, he was unmarked. Ali thought he had won nine rounds, but the best he could get from Referee Arthur Mercante was six, while Judge Artie Aidala awarded him the same, but Judge Bill Recht could give him only four. Ali intimated that the three officials had been influenced in their voting by his conviction and the fact that he was an active Black Muslim.

He also made a shrewd point when stating emphatically: "Guys who fight like Frazier won't be in boxing too long, though. Your body can't take that much punishment." Obviously he was referring to his big effort in round five when he stopped retreating before Frazier's blazing fists and

Dropped for only the third time in his career, Ali is floored by 'Smokin' Joe' and forced to take an 'eight' count in the 15th and final round.

bombarded his chin with precision punches, especially when Joe dropped his gloves and advanced bobbing and weaving, laughing at Ali and daring him to hit him.

Ali obliged, Frazier's knees buckled more than once, but Muhammad could not put down this human tank, who withstood a great deal more punishment in the sixth round when Ali tried hard to bring off his prediction and end the battle. Frazier absorbed more heavy and accurate shots in the ninth round, in one stretch taking as

many as eight blows to the head without landing a punch in return. He ignored the bombardment and whipped in a sizzling left hook to the jaw that almost put Ali down and sent him reeling back into the ropes.

There were whole rounds, however, when Muhammad did not land a blow of any significance, but spent the time in preventing Frazier from doing anything destructive. Ali would lean back on the ropes, wait for Joe to come in and then tie him up, so that all Frazier could do was to move his arms ineffectually. Or Ali would allow himself to be pinned in a corner, put up an elaborate defence and let his rival punch away at his arms and shoulders while keeping his head out of range. It was clever stuff, it was done to make Frazier look cheap, but it gained no scoring points for Ali. They were rounds he threw away and had only himself to blame for losing the verdict.

When he had left his dressing-room he had stated: "Now comes the moment of truth". It was about the best prophecy he had ever made. Later he was to make much of the fact that Frazier had spent several days in hospital after the contest, even though this was due to high blood pressure. Also, when Frazier eventually lost the championship in two rounds to George Foreman two years later, Ali claimed full responsibility by saying that he had softened up Smokin' Joe to such an extent that the first man to come along with a big punch would have no trouble in beating him easily.

9. The Great Comeback

For a short while there was talk of a return fight for the title between Ali and Frazier, but the champion dashed such hopes by announcing that he did not intend fighting again in 1971, but would concentrate on touring with his pop group, The Knockouts. Ali kept surprisingly quiet, except for stating that he had intended giving the Muslims a large donation from the proceeds of his fight with Frazier, but had not been able to do so because, after paying heavy taxes, he had been left with only 447,000 dollars (£197,000). By June he had decided to embark on another comeback campaign and signed to meet his former sparring-partner and ex-W.B.A. world champion, Jimmy Ellis, at Houston. Straight into the publicity scene came Ali to inform all and sundry that "Ellis once knocked me down in training. He brags about it. He also beat me once as an amateur and I beat him once. I'm glad to get him into the ring because he still thinks he can beat me."

All this was so much eye-wash, as was the report that he had broken with Angelo Dundee, the man who had trained him from the start of his pro career and been in his corner for every fight, even prodding him into leaving his corner for the round in which he won the world crown. Dundee was manager to Ellis. He suggested to Ali that as he could not be in two corners at one and the same time, he would like to be with his own fighter. This was agreed, but Muhammad allowed pressmen to say there had been a rift between them, it all added to the propaganda. A month before the Ellis fight, the U.S. Government gave the bout its biggest boost by announcing that Ali's conviction had been quashed officially on technical grounds, mainly because due heed had not been taken to his claims of being a conscientious objector at the time of his trial. In any case, as Ali was now 29, three years above the age for call-up, there seemed no point in letting the legal battle continue. He had won a fight as important to his career as any he had gained in the ring.

The bout with Ellis was scheduled for twelve-rounds and it ended with fifty seconds still to go, the referee intervening when Ellis had been staggered with a right to the head and was being battered with left and right hooks into a state of helplessness. Scaling his heaviest at 15 st. 10½ lbs., which gave him an advantage of 31½ lbs., Ali outboxed his former spar-mate all the way, had him rocking, but could not, or would not, put him down. Afterwards he declared that he could have knocked out Ellis, but did not want to. "I'm not out to kill anybody. I let him burn out his energy, while

I used the ring and defied him to hit me."

Joe Frazier, who watched the contest said: "Ellis fought a stupid fight. He did not know what to do. Ali is a big clown who came into the ring with over-sized trunks to hide his fat." This remark bore out the general impression that Muhammad had not been seriously concerned about the kind of opposition that Ellis could provide. It also demonstrated that even when below concert pitch, he could prevent an opponent from inflicting damage with his superlative defensive boxing skill.

Victory did not bring the anticipated return title fight with Frazier. While the world champion rested from the ring, Ali filled out the year with two further bouts, first outpointing Buster Mathis, a giant from Grand Rapids, Michigan, who had been inactive for $2\frac{1}{2}$ years. The bout, restricted to twelve-rounds, took place at the Houston Astrodome and was billed as "The Mountain comes to Muhammad". At 6 ft. 4 ins. and weighing 18 st. 4 lbs. Mathis was indeed mountainous, but Ali, scaling his heaviest yet at 16 st. 3 lbs. was no pigmy.

Again he treated the affair lightly, outboxing his man in every round. Mathis was both willing and game, but no match for Ali, who clowned and toyed with him. By the 11th Buster had been busted, was dropped twice and twice more in the final round, during which he was allowed to remain on his feet purely from sufferance on Muhammad's part. It was not a fight to excite the 21,000 onlookers and it virtually ended his popularity in the Texan town—he never fought there again during the next three years.

Ali rounded off 1971 by going to Ger-

many to score an easy win over top-ranking Jurgen Blin at the Hallenstadion in Zurich, knocking him out with a flurry of precision punches in round seven. In April of the following year, he travelled to Tokyo to outpoint Mac Foster, a Californian coloured heavy, over fifteen lackadaisical and disappointing rounds. In May he went to Vancouver to again outpoint George Chuvalo, this time over twelve rounds. It was another comfortable win, but unconvincing, and Ali's performance was far from the class needed for the proposed return contest with Frazier. In June Ali went back to Las Vegas and had no trouble in stopping former opponent Jerry Quarry in seven rounds, the referee intervening after 19 seconds when Muhammad pointed out that his rival was in no condition to take any further punishment.

If Ali was not causing sensations, he was building up a winning sequence and, incidentally, fighting his way back to physical perfection, his weight decreasing each time he went on the scales, while he could come out of fifteen rounds against a determined opponent without being out of breath. The circus continued in Dublin in July where Ali stopped sparring-partner Al Blue Lewis in eleven rounds, then came a more serious engagement in September when he climbed back into the Madison Square Garden ring to again face former champion, Floyd Patterson. No more sincere fighter than Patterson ever pulled on a pair of gloves. At 37 he was still trying to regain the crown he lost so easily to Sonny Liston. He asked for another set-to with Ali, maintaining that but for a back injury, he would have done better than he did when the pair first met

At Las Vegas, Ali was given stiffer opposition than expected when he met Joe Bugner, Britain's European heavyweight champion, during his 1971-1973 'comeback' campaign.

seven years previously and he had been stopped in twelve rounds.

It was a forlorn hope. Ali played with Patterson for a few rounds, then cut loose and gave him a sound thrashing, closing his left eye so completely that the ringside doctor ordered the referee to stop the one-sided contest when Floyd returned to his corner at the end of the seventh round. Winning his sixth contest of the year, Ali knocked out Bob Foster, the world light-heavyweight champion, in the eighth round at Stateline in Nevada, after flooring his opponent no less than seven times, but not before Foster had disturbed Ali's 'beauty' by slicing a cut under his left eye-

brow that required stitching.

While Muhammad had spent a busy and lucrative year, champion Frazier had engaged in two so-called defences of his title against un-rated boxers, Terry Daniels and Ron Stander, both of whom had been stopped in four rounds. Meanwhile, coming along at a fast and impressive pace was the 1968 Olympic Games heavyweight champion, George Foreman, from Marshall in Texas.

Ali celebrated his 31st birthday on January 17th, 1973. Five days later Foreman startled the fistic world by hammering Frazier to defeat in less than two rounds and all prospects of a return fight between

87

Muhammad and Smokin' Joe went up in smoke. But Ali continued to keep himself in fighting trim and in February took on Joe Bugner at Las Vegas, the bout being scheduled for twelve rounds.

Although an 8 to 1 underdog in the betting, the European champion stayed the distance, in spite of suffering a badly cut left eye as early as the first round. At 15 st. 9 lbs. Bugner outweighed his rival by 1¾ lbs., he also landed more left jabs than the coloured man had felt for a long time. But Ali's left was faster and smarter, he had vastly more experience, especially in the art of making a man miss. Hungarian-born Joe did rock his opponent with a right in round seven, but was not allowed to follow up his advantage as Ali kept well out of further trouble. Apart from this, the American had things pretty

much his own way and had won by a unanimous verdict at the finish.

Just 45 days later at San Diego he was in action again, this time opposed to Ken Norton, ranked ninth and intended to be just another stepping-stone in Ali's climb back to a heavyweight title fight. So he might have been but for a jolting right-hander that cracked Muhammad's jaw mid-way through the opening round. It was a critical injury that made the recipient concentrate even more than usual on defensive tactics, so that the aggressive Norton was the winner on a split decision at the finish, getting the vote of Referee Frank Rustich and Judge Hal Rickards, while Judge Fred Hayes—who was booed—gave it to Ali. The injured boxer spent the night in hospital where he underwent a 90-

In only the second defeat of his career, Ali was outpointed by Ken Norton and suffered a broken jaw at San Diego in March 1973. His conqueror, seen here taking a right-hander, at Inglewood, California.

minute operation, the crack which Norton had subsequently pounded into a clean break, having to be wired up. That he had fought 11½-rounds with a fractured jaw gave full evidence of Ali's gameness and pride, for afterwards it was revealed that Angelo Dundee had tried to persuade him to retire at the end of the second round.

It was a disheartening set-back and any ideas of an early fight with either Joe Frazier or George Foreman had to be abandoned. It was nearly six months before Muhammad was ready to fight again and he would hear of no other opponent than Norton, the pair meeting in Inglewood, California, again over the twelve rounds route. Ali got his revenge, but did not cover himself with glory, in fact, it was a split decision, with Referee Dick Young and Judge John Thomas voting for the former champion and Judge George Latka picking Norton.

Ali had trimmed down to 15 st. 2 lbs. after fifteen weeks of strenuous training and for the first six rounds outboxed his opponent with the greatest of ease. From then on he tired and his tough rival drove him into one corner after the other, putting in a sustained attack that many thought had wiped out Ali's earlier lead. Afterwards a weary-looking Muhammad told reporters that he had damaged his hand in the sixth round and when asked who would be his next opponent, he sighed and said; "I dunno, I'm too tired to think."

Forty-days later he was back in action, however, engaged in another 12-round bout, this time with Rudi Lubbers, a Dutchman listed fifth in the European ratings, a man who could not possibly give Ali more

Proud family man. Ali takes his daughter, Maryum, for a ride in August 1973. Picture was taken at Deer Park, Pennsylvania, when he was training for his return contest with Ken Norton.

Muhammad fights his way back into the role of leading challenger by outpointing Joe Frazier in the 'Fight of the Century' at New York, January 1974. Here he is boxing off an all-out assault from 'Smokin' Joe' in the latter stages of a memorable contest.

than a comfortable work-out. Staged at the Senyan Stadium in Jakarta in far-off Indonesia it was purely a television venture, the promoters being able to pay Ali a guarantee of 300,000 dollars, plus his expenses for a fortnight's stay prior to the contest, which was no more than an exhibition bout so far as the former champion was concerned.

With his advantage in height and weight, he scored an overwhelming victory without exerting himself for Lubbers was no threat and rarely landed a punch of any note from start to finish. Interviewed afterwards, unmarked Muhammad seemed displeased with his performance. "I am at the twilight

of my career", he admitted. "Every fight takes a lot out of me."

Did he believe this? I doubt it, because even before he accepted terms to fight Lubbers, he had signed to meet Joe Frazier again in Madison Square Garden, a match that the fistic world wanted and which everyone would regard as a final eliminator for the right to challenge George Foreman. The bout in Indonesia had been merely an exercise and in reality he was in better fighting shape than Smokin' Joe, who since losing his title had fought but once only, going to London to outpoint Joe Bugner over twelve rounds.

That was in July 1973 and the fight with Ali was scheduled for January 28, which denoted a six-month lay-off for Frazier, following another of the same period. During the year Ali had fought four times, but had not over-strained himself to get into perfect physical fitness. What sort of fight could be expected from two men who had already travelled fifteen punishing rounds, Frazier turned 30 and Ali past 32? They gave an exhilarating answer, putting up another tremendous battle that did the heavyweight situation a power of good.

Once again they packed the famous Garden to its limits, 20,748 fans paying 1,530,688 dollars. In addition there was the bonanza from the ancillary rights, sufficient to be able to pay each fighter three-million dollars and leave a satisfactory pile for the promoters. Weighing 212 pounds (15 st. 2 lbs.) which gave him an advantage of three pounds, Ali was favoured to win at the short odds of 8 to 5 and while he gained the vote of the referee and both judges, he had been given as hard a battle as when they first met three years previously. It was another classic display of fighter versus boxer, combining ferocity, skill, science and stamina, in fact, 36 minutes of intense warfare with no quarter asked and none given.

Ali's victory could be ascribed to one factor; he had learned from their earlier meeting, Frazier had not. Smokin' Joe adopted the self-same tactics, a steady, merciless, advancing attack, with the single object of hammering his opponent to the canvas. Muhammad used the ring just as much as before, his defence was superb and the way he nullified his strong rival's non-stop aggression was masterful. But in addition he changed his counter-punches from left jabs and right crosses to the head, to whipping uppercuts that whistled through Frazier's fast working gloves and connected with his granite chin. That he could take Frazier's savage hooks to the head when they got through and endure his heavy swings to the body, spoke volumes for his fine physical condition. The same could be said for his opponent, who found Ali a far harder hitter this time, particularly with the left and right hooks he exploded on Joe's jaw as he came forward with the persistence of a tank.

Here were two former world heavy-weight champions fighting determinedly for the right to regain the coveted title. There were no prolonged periods of nega-tive fighting as there had been in their first encounter. Now it was total war, with pure savagery on one side and skill, combined with intent, on the other. There was no time for skirmishing, Frazier was unrelent-ing, and Ali dare not lose concentration for a single moment.

At no time was Smokin' Joe in serious trouble, he merely grinned when caught by a shaking punch; whereas Muhammad had to get over bad times in the fifth, eighth and tenth rounds, when he was caught with savage left hooks that had him reeling into the ropes, forcing him to bring out every defensive artifice in his extensive repertoire to prevent himself from being floored. But, in the opinion of most onlookers Ali won six rounds by clear margins, although Judge Jack Gordon gave him eight and Judge Tony Castellano favoured him with seven. Referee Tony Perez scored it six to Ali, five to Frazier with one even. Few of the spectators quarrelled with the decision and Smokin' Joe's features, an ugly mass of bumps and bruises, were befitting a loser, whereas the winner came out relatively unmarked.

The way was now cleared for the in-evitable championship fight with George Foreman, six years junior to Ali, and a far heavier hitter. Of course, he was lacking in experience, having participated in only forty bouts as a professional, but he had an unbeaten record, with all his wins, bar one, being gained in a few rounds. He had pounded iron-man Frazier to destruction in less than two rounds at Kingston in Jamaica in January 1973, knocked out Joe (King) Roman in a single round in Tokyo, and flattened Ken Norton, Ali's one-time conqueror, in two rounds at Caracas in Venezuela, on March 26, 1974. That meant that his three world title bouts had lasted barely five rounds, and there were many critics ready to label the Mexico Olympics Champion as the hardest hitting heavyweight in the world.

Television had taken big boxing into hitherto the most unlikely places in the world and when it was announced that the Foreman *v* Ali clash would be staged at Kinshasa in Zaire under the sponsorship of the government of that new country, no one raised an eyebrow. It was anticipated that the over-all takings for this eagerly-awaited meeting would amount to thirty-million dollars, of which each boxer would take five-million, this colossal amount being put up by Risnelia, a Swiss company acting on behalf of the Zaire government. It was a high price to pay for the privilege of being the first African nation to stage a world heavyweight boxing championship, but a fine publicity follow-up to the entry of their footballers into the World Cup competition.

As the fight had to be sold to the rest of the world, particularly the United States, all the available publicity was more than welcome and, as usual, Ali could be relied upon to contribute more than his share. There were pre-fight prophecies and threats that blew up into a serious affair when the pair met as guests at the annual New York Boxing Writers' dinner held in the Starlight Roof of the Waldorf-Astoria hotel on June 26, 1974 with three months yet to go to the championship contest. Nothing untoward happened until Ali, a featured speaker, turned a sarcastic tongue on Foreman, making pointed and derogatory remarks, until the recognised champion could stand no more. Going to the microphone, he told the assembly: "I don't know how you people can stand this. I'm leaving".

George picked up a plaque that had been presented to him as Fighter of the Year, but Ali grabbed it and held it behind his back. At once there was a scuffle. Foreman, trying to regain his trophy, ripped Ali's dinner jacket, whereupon Muhammad retaliated by tearing George's coat and ripping off his shirt. They hurled abuse at each other with Ali screaming: "I'm going to beat your Christian ass, you white, flag-waving bitch, you", the last being a blasting reference to the patriotic gesture made by Foreman on the rostrum at the Olympic Games when, after receiving his gold medal, he waved a small Stars and Stripes to the cheering spectators. Four members of Ali's entourage held him back, but he struggled free to pick up wine-glasses and hurl them in Foreman's direction. Eventually they were separated and when George had gone home, Ali, realising that this time he had gone too far, made some form of apology by insisting that he had only been fooling around.

Weeks before the scheduled date of September 25, both fighters took up training quarters in Zaire, with Foreman staying at a modern American-style hotel that looked down on Kinshasa from its highest vantage point, while Ali located himself at N'sele, a quiet state holiday centre forty miles from the city. Things went along smoothly until, with a week to go, Foreman sustained an eye injury when engaged in a sparring session with Bill McMurray. The latter had been instructed to move fast and use the ring in imitation of Muhammad and somehow his elbow collided with the champion's right eye, causing a cut between the eyelid and the eyebrow.

The wound was sufficient to cause a five

week's postponement and in consequence, a major setback to those who were financially interested in the project. The new date was October 30, the fight to start at dawn in the vast 60,000 seater May 20 Stadium. The weigh-in took place on the Saturday previous in the ring in which the title fight was to be fought, with 15,000 onlookers, and it must be said that for once Ali had to take a back seat, mainly because he had talked himself hoarse in the pre-fight interviews.

He had been greeted by a great volume of cheering accompanied by cries of 'Kill him, Ali', but Foreman's entry was extremely impressive. He marched in, head high like a world-beater, his height of 6 ft. 3½ ins., plus his massive muscularity, making him look the bigger of the pair. At 15 st. 10 lbs., he was the heavier by four pounds, but statistics showed that he was shorter in the reach by 3½ ins. Still standing on the scales, he lifted one arm upright, then the other and, inflating his chest, looked like a mighty ebony statue that brought forth a roar from the big crowd. Ali made no such gesture, nor was there any attempt at clowning. With his biggest publicity weapon subdued, he had to take second place. It was Foreman who received the greatest ovation as he strode back to the dressing-rooms.

As for the fight, it was almost a case of master versus novice. Ali drew his rival's fangs in the first five rounds, cleverly drawing him into a non-stop attack, the potency of which he robbed by skilfully moving just that fraction out of range. There was no butterfly dancing round the ring this time, no fooling, no taking chances, no daring, suicidal openings, but a concentrated yet simple display of the art of self-defence, during which Foreman gradually sapped himself of his stamina, strength and confidence. Time after time he tossed the big punches that had flattened Frazier and so many others, but Ali was never there to receive them and if he was, the bulk of George's blows were intercepted by adroitly placed gloves, forearms, elbows, biceps, or shoulders, whether aimed at the head or the body.

Only in the second and fifth rounds did the excited spectators get the idea that Foreman was about to break through and batter his ageing rival to the boards, but at each critical moment, Ali remained cool and either moved out of danger, or closed in to hold his opponent in a vice-like grip that rendered him temporarily harmless, or hold out a long arm and press down George's head and reduce him to impotency. By the sixth round it was obvious that Ali was dictating the battle and now Foreman was taking heavy punishment as Muhammad sharpened his blows and caught the oncoming champion with punches that left their mark on his face or crashed into his body to make his legs shake.

By the eighth round George was lumbering round, still following his elusive rival, but in a hopeless daze, with little idea of what to do next. All the time Ali was taunting his inadequacy and midway through the round, in the manner in which the toreador dispatches the bull, the challenger decided that the time was right for the finish. A flurry of wicked double-handed hooks to the chin had Foreman open for the 'kill' and it came in the form of a downward power-packed right that struck the angle of the jaw and sent the recipient

(*Above*) Ali becomes the second man to twice win the world's heavyweight title when he knocked out giant George Foreman in the 8th round at Kinshasa, Zaire, in October 1974. It was a tremendous performance for a man in his 33rd year.

headlong to the canvas to roll over on to his back, his right knee bent, his senses scattered, the dazed look of bewilderment on his face. At the count of 'six' he lifted his head and stared at his corner. His chief second signalled him to rise at 'eight' but it was a feat beyond the powers of the stricken fighter, who was striving desperately to pull himself into the upright when the 'out' was called.

Immediately the ringside reporters and the television commentators were telling the world that Muhammad Ali had won the heavyweight championship of the world for the second time, thus equalling the record set up by Floyd Patterson in 1960.

In the opinion of most of the fistic fraternity, he had also proved to be what he had always claimed—The Greatest of all the World Heavyweight Champions.

(*Left*) The Greatest? In the ring most certainly and his full-voiced action (with musical accompaniment) is certainly shown here!

Fighting Record of Muhammad Ali
(Cassius Clay)

Born at Louisville, Kentucky, U.S.A. January 17th, 1942

1960. National American Athletic Union light-heavyweight champion.
National Golden Gloves Heavyweight Champion, U.S.A.
Olympic Games light-heavyweight gold medallist at Rome.

PROFESSIONAL RECORD

Date	Opponent	Verdict	Venue
1960			
Oct. 29	Tunney Hunsaker	w.pts. 6	Louisville
Dec. 27	Herb Siler	w.ko. 4	Miami
1961			
Jan. 17	Tony Esperti	w.rsf. 3	Miami
Feb. 7	Jim Robinson	w.rsf. 1	Miami
Feb. 21	Donnie Fleeman	w.rsf. 7	Miami
Apl. 19	Lamar Clark	w.ko. 2	Louisville
Jun. 26	Duke Sabedong	w.pts. 10	Las Vegas
Jul. 22	Alonzo Johnson	w.pts. 10	Louisville
Oct. 7	Alex Miteff	w.rsf. 6	Louisville
Nov. 29	Willi Besmanoff	w.rsf. 7	Louisville
1962			
Feb. 19	Sonny Banks	w.rsf. 4	New York
Feb. 28	Don Warner	w.rsf. 4	Miami
Apl. 23	George Logan	w.rsf. 4	Los Angeles
May 19	Billy Daniels	w.rsf. 7	New York
Jul. 20	Alejandro Lavorante	w.ko. 5	Los Angeles
Nov. 15	Archie Moore	w.rsf. 4	Los Angeles
1963			
Jan. 24	Charley Powell	w.ko. 3	Pittsburgh
Mar. 13	Doug Jones	w.pts. 10	New York
Jun. 18	Henry Cooper	w.rsf. 5	London
1964			
Feb. 25	*Sonny Liston	w.ret. 6	Miami

(*Heavyweight Championship of the World*)

1965			
May 25	*Sonny Liston	w.ko. 1	Lewiston
Nov. 22	*Floyd Patterson	w.rsf. 12	Las Vegas
1966			
Mar. 29	*George Chuvalo	w.pts. 15	Toronto
May 21	*Henry Cooper	w.rsf. 6	London
Aug. 6	*Brian London	w.ko. 3	London
Sep. 10	*Karl Mildenberger	w.rsf. 12	Frankfurt
Nov. 14	*Cleveland Williams	w.rsf. 3	Houston
1967			
Feb. 6	*Ernie Terrell	w.pts. 15	Houston
Mar. 22	*Zora Folley	w.ko. 7	New York
1968–1969	Inactive—Forfeited title		
1970			
Oct. 26	Jerry Quarry	w.rsf. 3	Atlanta
Dec. 7	Oscar Bonavena	w.rsf. 15	New York
1971			
Mar. 8	*Joe Frazier	l.pts. 15	New York
Jul. 26	Jimmy Ellis	w.rsf. 12	Houston
Nov. 17	Buster Mathis	w.pts. 12	Houston
Dec. 26	Jurgen Blin	w.ko. 7	Zurich
1972			
Apl. 1	Mac Foster	w.pts. 15	Tokyo
May 1	George Chuvalo	w.pts. 12	Vancouver
Jun. 29	Jerry Quarry	w.rsf. 7	Las Vegas
Jul. 19	Al (Blue) Lewis	w.rsf. 11	Dublin
Sep. 20	Floyd Patterson	w.rsf. 7	New York
Nov. 21	Bob Foster	w.ko. 8	Stateline
1973			
Feb. 14	Joe Bugner	w.pts. 12	Las Vegas
Mar. 31	Ken Norton	l.pts. 12	San Diego
Sep. 10	Ken Norton	w.pts. 12	Inglewood
Oct. 20	Rudi Lubbers	w.pts. 12	Jakarta
1974			
Jan. 28	Joe Frazier	w.pts. 12	New York
Oct. 30	*George Foreman	w.ko. 8	Kinshasa, Zaire
	(*Regained world heavyweight title*)		

* World heavyweight title fight   w.pts.—won on points
w.rsf.—won stopped by referee.   w.ko.—won by knockout